Praise for

HOW SCHOOLS WORK

"[Duncan] comes across on every page as smart, honest, decent, articulate, knowledgeable, humble, and deeply caring. Who could wish for a better advocate for the children many of our schools are failing every day or for a country whose schools are falling further and further behind those in other industrialized countries?"

—*Education Week*

"Arne Duncan was one of the most powerful education secretaries in US history. Which is not to say he got his way. In this surprisingly candid chronology of his lifelong quest to fix America's schools, Duncan reveals how he learned to run toward angry parents (not away from them), to understand the cowardice of certain national politicians (and the courage of others), and to hear the lies that get told about our education system (including a couple that he told himself)."

—Amanda Ripley, *New York Times* bestselling author
of *The Smartest Kids in the World*

"In *How Schools Work*, Secretary Duncan outlines an honest and thoughtful way forward for our education system. This book merits every American's serious consideration because, as Secretary Duncan explains, our children, our economy, and our national security are at stake."

—Vice President Joe Biden

"The book exudes an earnest *Leave It to Beaver* charm. . . . [Duncan shares] moving accounts of his experiences with the families of students killed by gun violence. He shows admirable verve in describing his success working with a Chicago school system lawyer to find a contractual workaround to make an afterschool program logistically feasible, and his later willingness, as superintendent, to give *Freakonomics* researcher Steven Levitt access to the city's test data in order to flag teacher cheating."

—*Education Next*

"Former Education Secretary Arne Duncan makes a powerful case in his new book, *How Schools Work*, that major increases in teacher pay, coupled with true accountability and multiple measures for reducing gun violence in schools, stand at the top of any to-do list to improve American education."

—Brookings

"Duncan's experienced perspective will interest anyone invested in American public education."

—*Publishers Weekly*

HOW
SCHOOLS
WORK

An Inside Account *of* Failure *and* Success
from One *of the* Nation's Longest-Serving
Secretaries *of* Education

ARNE DUNCAN

SIMON & SCHUSTER PAPERBACKS
New York   London   Toronto   Sydney   New Delhi

AUTHOR'S NOTE: This book is a memoir about the many years I've spent working in the world of American education. Some of what's found in these pages is based on recollection and not recordings or documentation; accordingly, certain names and places have been changed.

Simon & Schuster Paperbacks
1230 Avenue of the Americas
New York, NY 10020

First Simon & Schuster trade paperback edition August 2019

SIMON & SCHUSTER and colophon are registered trademarks of Simon & Schuster, Inc.

For information about special discounts for bulk purchases, please contact Simon & Schuster Special Sales at 1-866-506-1949 or business@simonandschuster.com.

The Simon & Schuster Speakers Bureau can bring authors to your live event. For more information or to book an event, contact the Simon & Schuster Speakers Bureau at 1-866-248-3049 or visit our website at www.simonspeakers.com.

Interior design by Ruth Lee-Mui

Manufactured in the United States of America

10   9   8   7   6   5   4   3   2   1

Library of Congress Cataloging-in-Publication Data.
Names: Duncan, Arne, author. Title: How schools work : an inside account from one of the nation's longest-serving secretaries of education / Arne Duncan. Description: First Simon & Schuster hardcover edition. | New York : Simon & Schuster, [2018] | Includes bibliographical references and index. Identifiers: LCCN 2018016716 (print) | LCCN 2018028092 (ebook) | ISBN 9781501173073 (Ebook) | ISBN 9781501173059 (hardcover : alk. paper) Subjects: LCSH: Education—Aims and objectives—United States. | Education and state—United States. | Public schools—United States. | Educational change—United States. | Duncan, Arne. | School administrators—United States—Biography. | Cabinet officers—United States—Biography. Classification: LCC LA217.2 (ebook) | LCC LA217.2 .D86 2018 (print) | DDC 379.0973—dc23. LC record available at https://lccn.loc.gov/2018016716

ISBN 978-1-5011-7305-9
ISBN 978-1-5011-7306-6 (pbk)
ISBN 978-1-5011-7307-3 (ebook)

To Karen, Claire, and Ryan: thank you for inspiring me every day, and for walking every step of this journey with me.

To my extended family and friends: thank you for all your support and love—you mean more to me than I can ever express.

To everyone who works to educate and nurture children: we all owe you a debt we can never repay. Thank you for your service.

CONTENTS

LIES, LIES EVERYWHERE

Education runs on lies. That's probably not what you'd expect from a former secretary of education, but it's the truth. How schools work best is often by confronting and fighting these lies, but this is exhausting and sometimes perilous work usually undertaken by an isolated teacher or principal. So, the lies persist. They are as emblematic of our system as an apple left on the corner of a favorite teacher's desk. But, unlike the apple, the lies aren't sweet. They are overripe and rotten.

I've been aware of education's lies since childhood: I saw them every day at an after-school program that my mom, Sue Duncan, ran on Chicago's South Side—but as a child I never fully appreciated how insidious they were. That began to change when I got to know someone named Calvin Williams.

That fall I was set to begin my senior year at Harvard, where I studied sociology and co-captained the Crimson basketball team. Like many young people who have the good fortune to get an elite college education, I was trying to figure out what to do with my life. (I got into Harvard through elbow grease and athletic skill, and the only reason I could afford it was because my dad's employer, the University of Chicago, paid most of the tuition.) Many of my friends were going into law or investment banking, and I considered these too. But I wanted to test myself. I wanted to figure out whether the work my mom did was only a piece of me, or if it was truly who I was.

And then there was basketball.

Even though my Harvard team wasn't very good—we won nine games against seventeen losses in my final season—I had a decent game and I hoped to play professionally, if not in the NBA, then perhaps overseas. I was young and I needed to at least *try* to play ball professionally, didn't I? It had been my childhood dream, after all. Still, I knew basketball wouldn't last forever and that someday I'd need to make use of the opportunities granted by a Harvard education. The question remained: would education be my life's calling after basketball?

If my experiences at the Sue Duncan Children's Center were any indication, the answer was probably yes. For more than twenty-five years my mom had been helping kids in the North Kenwood/Oakland neighborhood get their educations. From three in the afternoon to eight at night she worked to make up for what the local schools couldn't or wouldn't teach between eight and three. My brother and sister and I had also grown up at her after-school program, and I knew that it was the perfect place to explore whether I wanted to work in education later in life. So, I took a year off after my junior year—which was practically unheard-of at Harvard—and went to work in her program while simultaneously doing fieldwork for my senior sociology thesis. The year was 1986.

I spent most of that year working with older kids, sixteen- and seventeen-year-olds who were preparing for the ACT, or with kids who wanted to finish high school strong so they could have a shot at a decent-paying job. It was a hard time in life for these teenagers, many of whom sat around and talked about whether it was possible for them to live past thirty. This was not something I sat around and talked about with my friends at Harvard; we all expected to live and hoped to thrive.

One of the neighborhood kids who walked through the center's doors that July was Calvin Williams.

I'd known the Williams family for years. They lived less than a block away from the Kenwood-Ellis Church, where my mom's program was located. Like nearly every kid in the neighborhood, Calvin was African American; but unlike many kids, his family was intact. He had two brothers, and all of them lived at home with their mom and dad, who both toiled away at working-class jobs. Most families in North Kenwood/Oakland were broken and scattered, without fathers or with siblings divided among aunts and uncles, grandmothers and grandfathers. Not the Williamses, though. They were seemingly immune to the violence and gang activity that hung over the neighborhood like a cloud, darkening everything that happened on the streets and in homes.

(This cloud also hung over my mom's program. Once, in 1970, when I was only five, the center was located in the nearby Woodlawn Mennonite Church, but had to be relocated after the minister, Reverend Curtis Burrell, refused to allow a gang called the Blackstone Rangers to use it as an arsenal to store their guns. The punishment for that refusal was the Rangers firebombing the church, which thankfully they did at night when the building was unoccupied. No one was hurt, but the fire fatally compromised the building and my mom was forced to move out with what she could salvage. One of my earliest memories was of shuttling boxes of books from Woodlawn over to Kenwood-Ellis Church, where the center was still located in 1986. Another time years later, we were driving down a street a few blocks from the center to pick up one of her students. The car was full of kids and, like always, Sue ambled along at about ten miles per hour. But on that day, someone jumped in front of us with an assault rifle and aimed past the car at the older brother of the kid we were picking up. My mom jammed the brakes, threw our station wagon in reverse, and screamed away as fast as the car would go, probably thirty-five or forty miles per hour. No one got shot and no one was hurt that time either. To this day we still laugh that by far the fastest we ever saw her drive was going backward!)

One summer day I found myself sitting on the church steps, waiting for Calvin. The church, a gray Romanesque fortress of a building, its high-peaked gable end facing Greenwood Avenue, had stood watch over the neighborhood for more than one hundred years. Like any structure that manages to survive that long in an American city, Kenwood-Ellis had witnessed a lot of change, from the neighborhood's early days as a leafy enclave for wealthy Chicagoans to the neighborhood's current state as a mostly neglected black ghetto. My family lived in a small house less than two miles away, on the other side of the Forty-Seventh Street divide, in the racially mixed, middle-class neighborhood of Hyde Park. I'd walked to the church that day, a stroll that took barely thirty minutes. It's a strange feature of cities, how quickly they can change from block to block. My family was solidly middle-class—it's not like I was living in some walled-off community—but Calvin and I might as well have lived on opposite ends of the state of Illinois.

I specifically remember the heat that day as I caught sight of Calvin striding up Forty-Sixth Street. I was in the shade but it was humid and no breeze came off the lake to the east. I waved when Calvin was about a half a block away. He smiled and waved back before breaking into a light jog. He looked happy. He looked eager.

The Williams boys were great kids who stayed out of trouble and in school. They didn't drink or smoke and they got good grades. They were on track to grow up and live decent lives. Maybe they'd get out of the South Side, maybe they'd choose to stay, but whatever happened, all signs indicated that the Williams boys had a better chance at succeeding than many of their neighbors.

However, the most important thing about Calvin was that he could really play ball.

He was seventeen in 1986 and was easily twice the player I'd been at his age. He was long, lithe, and quick, had a good shot and better instincts on both ends of the court. I'd played pickup games with him; he was fun to play with and let his game talk for him. He was one of those players who made things easier for teammates and a hell of a lot harder for opponents. I had three years of college ball under my belt, and it was obvious that Calvin's future college career had a lot more upside than mine ever did. He'd always been a good student, consistently making the B honor roll a few blocks away at Martin Luther King High School, where his Jaguars had gone 32 and 1 in '86 and won the Illinois State AA Championship.

Bottom line: his game was good enough to earn a scholarship to a rarefied program at a Division I school. All we had to do was get him up to par on his test-taking skills so that he could get a decent score on the ACT.

"Hey, Arne!" Calvin said, stopping at the bottom of the church steps. He was in the sun, I was in the shade. "What's up?"

"Nothing. Just trying to stay cool. You?"

"Same, man. It's hotter than you know what out here."

Chicagoans love to complain about the temperature no matter the season. Too hot in the summer, too cold the rest of the year. Cry us a river.

"Have you thought about what we talked about last time?" I asked. "About where you want to go for college?"

"Honestly, since school's out, it's all I think of," he said. "Coach was saying I could aim high for Kansas, Kentucky, Georgia Tech. I was thinking maybe Illinois too, just to stay close to home. I don't know where else. 'Cuse, maybe? They were good last year."

"I think it might be colder there than here," I joked.

"Yeah, maybe. More snow, I think. That's what they say, anyway."

I stood and stretched out my arms, my T-shirt clinging to my shoulders. Snow was the furthest thing from my mind at that moment. "You're good enough for any of those places, that's for sure," I said.

"I guess, man. Not good enough for *Harvard*, though," he said with a snicker.

"Are you kidding? You'd destroy the entire Ivy League by yourself. They wouldn't be able to keep up." I spoke the truth. There wasn't a player in the Ivies who could stay in front of him. Not on the break, not in the half court, not bursting off of a pick and roll. No one. "I'm not going to let you waste your time at a place like Harvard." I turned toward the church door. "Come on, let's get started."

The church didn't have air-conditioning in those days but the stone walls kept the inside a little cooler, especially in the early part of summer. By the end of August, after it had cooked for a couple of months, it would be hotter, but for now it was comfortable.

Calvin followed me up a rickety flight of stairs to the second floor. The classrooms there were arranged by age, a couple of them subdivided into smaller learning areas. The room for little kids had tables and chairs that were low to the ground, a cushioned reading area with some matted stuffed animals, a place to draw and cut out shapes from donated magazines or construction paper, and a place to lay out colored blocks that Sue used to teach math concepts. The area for older kids a couple doors down was less kid-like. The desks were normal height, and the motley collection of wooden and plastic chairs were all made for adults, even if kids like Calvin were still getting taller and longer. (I shuddered to think of where his game would go if he grew two or three more inches.) Books were piled everywhere in a seemingly haphazard arrangement, but one that my mom knew inside and out. On the walls were posters of inspirational figures: people you'd expect, like Martin Luther King, Mark Twain, Abraham Lincoln, Langston Hughes, and Mahatma Gandhi, but also people who were local to the Kenwood/Hyde Park area—Muhammad Ali, Carol Moseley Braun, Edward H. Levi, and Muddy Waters. The message with this latter group was simple: *Great people come from here. You can be great too.*

Calvin and I sat at a regular school table with a pale linoleum top that was cool to the touch. I'd arrived a little earlier and already set out materials. This would be our first time working together, so I needed to get an idea of where he needed the most help. I was giving him what today I'd call an assessment, but which back then I just called a reading packet.

The packet replicated the English comprehension section of a standardized test like the ACT. There was a passage—a piece of fiction from an old book or an article from a periodical—followed by some basic questions. Calvin would have to write out his answers, so I'd set out a couple of sharpened No. 2 pencils and a short stack of loose-leaf paper. I made sure he was comfortable, watched him read the passage and the first question, and left him to write while I got us some ice water from the kitchen downstairs.

When I came back I set his glass on the table. I looked over his shoulder at his work. He'd answered about five questions already. He took a break, looked up at me, smiling, and said, "Thanks for the water, man. I'm thirsty as hell." "Hell" is about as tame as they come, but this was one of the few times I heard Calvin swear, including on the court, where foul language blares constantly. He picked up his glass and drank all the water in three or four loud gulps.

I didn't drink. Instead I stood there, frozen solid like the ice in my glass. I was shocked. I plainly saw that Calvin struggled to read and could barely form a proper sentence. His letters were fine but his spelling was dismal. His ability to craft a cohesive thought using written language was nonexistent. I wasn't an expert, but if I had to guess, Calvin Williams, a rising high school senior on the B honor roll, could read and write at a second- or third-grade level.

"You all right, man?" he asked.

"Yeah. Fine." I took a sip from my water, hoping the cold ice clinking on my teeth would jolt me out of it.

Calvin looked down at the page, then back up at me. "I do something wrong?"

I sat down next to him. "Nah, nothing." I put a finger on the words he'd written out. "You write much at school?"

He shrugged. "Guess so. I got a B-minus in English at the end of the year. Passed the tests and all."

I didn't know what to say. I knew automatically that, barring some miracle, I would not be able to give Calvin ten years of English instruction in two or three months. I knew in my heart, and as much as I wished it otherwise, that he had no chance of ever getting into a Division I school. He probably wouldn't score higher than 12 or 13 on his ACT: the absolute minimum for getting into college was 16, and that was still incredibly low.

"We have a lot of work to do, Calvin."

"This ain't good?"

"It's . . . Look, I'm not going to lie to you. If you want to go to Kansas or Syracuse or any of those other places, we have to get down to work. And we'll have to work hard, all summer long."

He kind of chuckled. "All right, no problem. That's why I'm here, ain't it? You know I'll put it in."

I did know it. He was an easy kid, a joy. He worked hard at basketball and he'd work hard here too. He wasn't lying.

But *I* was. It hit me so hard. The odds of him living out his dreams were close to zero—and why? He hadn't screwed up. He hadn't joined a gang or started drinking. He hadn't ended up in juvenile hall for some stupid teenage transgression. He hadn't become a teenage father. He was a model kid who'd done everything right. His talent for basketball would be all for nothing. Not because he had failed or his family had failed, but because the education system had failed. Calvin Williams wouldn't make it because of the lies that the Chicago schools had told him and his parents about how much he'd learned, and about how ready he was for college. The truth, though, was that he'd learned far too little, and he wasn't ready.

We did work hard that summer, sometimes seven days a week. The more I learned about what he didn't know, the more depressing the whole exercise became. In math, Calvin had to begin with fractions, which was what fifth and sixth graders did. He knew almost nothing on the social studies section of the ACT. I remember him saying, "I do good in history, but either that stuff isn't in our books, or we skipped that section, or something." He couldn't answer any questions that dealt with science. Also, he didn't know he was allowed to write in the test booklet. Calvin thought part of the test was having to do all the math problems in his head. He was amazed when I told him he could work them out right there in the book.

Through all of this I didn't give up on him, but I also never had the courage to tell him straight up that he wouldn't be going to college. I'm not proud of that. I've fallen out of touch with Calvin over the years, and I'm not sure when it dawned on him that he wouldn't be going to some big-time program, but if I had to guess it was probably when his ACT scores came back later that year.

My mom always liked to get the kids young. She knew she could change the life of a five-year-old but that changing the life of an older kid was a lot harder. With Calvin, we were too late. If he'd come into the center as a sixth grader, then he would have been more than fine. But not as an eleventh grader. The hole was too deep, and the timeline was too short. Yes, he worked hard. Yes, he improved. Yes, we helped him. But it wasn't close to enough.

"This ain't good?" he innocently asked that first day. This question haunted me for years, and in some ways it still does. The worst part of the whole thing was that *he didn't know what he didn't know*. He truly thought he was a B honor roll student. He was as certain about this as about the fact that he was a gifted athlete with a bright future. He had simply been passed through the system. Did this happen because he was a good kid? Or because he was a star basketball player? Or because he was a black kid from the inner city for whom there were no real academic expectations? I don't know, but what I do know is that he'd been lied to his entire life. The lies were so ingrained and had been told for so long that they'd become invisible. The whole thing was so needlessly cruel. Here was a young man who represented the best of what we had on the South Side, and we as adults had given him our worst. Why? Because, unlike me, he came up on the wrong side of Forty-Seventh Street. Those twelve blocks from my house changed everything.

I returned to Harvard that fall and finished my undergrad studies. My senior thesis was all about kids like Calvin and about my mom's program, in which I had the good fortune to grow up and learn, not just about what was in books, but about what was on the basketball court, about what was on the streets, and about what was in people. My thesis was, in part, about the lie I told Calvin Williams that hot summer afternoon.

I ended up playing professional basketball for a few years after I graduated, although in Australia and not the NBA. (I did manage to get invited—and cut—from camp with the Celtics.) I played for two years in Melbourne and for another two in Tasmania, where I met my wife. Since returning from that faraway place, I've devoted my life and career to helping kids. I've tried to make the American educational system better functioning and more honest. For me this work has been all about closing that achievement gap between where I grew up and where Calvin grew up. It's been about trying to erase the Forty-Seventh Street divide, which exists all across the country, from the densest cities to the most sparsely populated rural areas. In America, there's no reason that a kid born in one place should not have the same chances and opportunities as a kid born in another. This work has not been easy. I have seen the lies challenged at many turns, but they survive. They persist.

The lies told to Calvin were not told to torture him. They were not intended to make children's lives worse, or to demoralize parents, or to make America less competitive or less intelligent. They didn't exist with the purpose of turning poor kids into poor adults. More often than not they existed to protect resources, or to safeguard jobs, or to control what kids were taught and how or whether they were tested on what they knew. Nearly all of the lies had to do with money and where power was concentrated, not with education. This was the case then, and in too many places it's still the case now. The big lies are the ones that the system tells to parents about how their kids are learning—the ones that schools tell to every level of government about how great their students are doing. In turn, these government offices tell families and students that their children are well prepared to grow up and graduate into an increasingly complex, technically challenging, and highly competitive world. The truth is that, compared to students in other countries, far too few of our kids actually are prepared. These are the lies that create students like Calvin Williams.

Are we coming up short everywhere? Absolutely not. I'm not throwing the entire system under the school bus. Despite the issue of gun violence, schools are safe havens, and there are countless K–12 public schools in this country, in every single state, where great leaders and teachers buck trends and where resources are concentrated, laser-like, on doing right by students. Some states, like Massachusetts and Tennessee, have made hard decisions that have paid tremendous dividends for the children of their states. But the existence of these schools and statewide initiatives does not exonerate those other schools or states that are not up to par, nor does their existence help with the problems of perception. Time and again I've seen how schools suffer from something we might call the "Congress polling problem." This is the phenomenon that results when voters are asked to rate Congress, which they invariably grade poorly, and are then asked to rate their own congressperson, whom they rate as satisfactory or higher. The same thing happens when Americans are polled about schools: "Oh, the nation's schools are in big trouble, but ours are pretty good!" If the latter were true everywhere, then how can the former also be true? It can't. This is the definition of "cognitive dissonance," and it is harming the country as a whole.

The "good" schools in this country haven't managed to defeat the lies that undermine our system so much as they've been able to circumvent them. Too many of our schools have not been able to do this. This is true across the United States. But if the story of Calvin Williams was the most poignant in spurring me toward a life in education, then the story of John Easton and his damning PowerPoint presentation was the most alarming. It wouldn't happen for many years to come, but it compelled me to push ahead and, eventually, to try to upend the system entirely.

IF WE BUILD IT, THEY WILL COME

In 1987, less than a year after I tried in vain to help Calvin Williams realize his dreams, William Bennett, Ronald Reagan's secretary of education, famously called Chicago's public schools "the worst in the nation." He went on to say that it would take "a man or woman of steel"—a superhero—to clean up our schools.

I'm not that superhero. Far from it. And it wouldn't take only one man or woman of steel—rather it would take a whole Justice League of educational superstars. However, Secretary Bennett did have a point. Throughout the '70s and '80s Chicago's system suffered from a raft of issues, from white flight to frequent teachers' strikes, from plummeting graduation rates to soaring truancy, from chronic corruption to fiscal inefficiencies. The problems were systemic and felt intractable. In 1988 the Illinois state legislature passed a law decentralizing school control, granting significant powers to local school boards. For several years these boards were locally elected; in Chicago the board consisted of twenty-three members, five of whom were appointed by the mayor. It was a system that fractured the landscape, creating fiefdoms that fought over unequal slices cut from the same pie. One district's gain was invariably another district's loss. It did not make for easy or efficient governing.

That changed in 1994. If there was ever a superhero in the struggle to improve the lives of Chicago's children, then it would have to have been the city's forty-third mayor, Richard M. Daley. And it didn't hurt that he came with a committed and more-than-able sidekick: his wife, Maggie Daley.

Mayor Daley, who came to office in 1989 and would win a record six consecutive terms, gained control of the schools when the state legislature in Springfield passed the Chicago School Reform Amendatory Act in 1995. The law centralized control with the mayor's office, giving Daley the power to trim the school board's size and appoint *all* of its members. This created a chain of command and accountability that ran directly to the mayor, who could look at the system as a whole and be judged by voters as to his success or failure. The Republican-controlled state legislature probably thought they were hanging Daley, a Democrat, with problems he couldn't solve. They probably thought that the people of Chicago would eventually deem Daley a failure on schools, and they'd make him pay some future electoral price.

It didn't quite work out that way. Whether Daley wanted school control or not, he embraced it. He rechristened the board of education's superintendent its chief executive officer, picking the city budget director, Paul Vallas, to take the helm. Within a year Paul had balanced the budget, signed a new four-year contract with the teachers' union, and undertaken the heavy lifting of rehabilitating the many school buildings across the city that were falling into ruin.

A few years later, in 1998, I joined Chicago Public Schools (CPS), technically working for Vallas but not yet reporting to him. It was not a decision I made lightly. After seeing all the harm the school system had done to Chicago's poorer kids, I considered CPS to be the enemy. But the fact that Mayor Daley had taken control gave me a glimmer of hope. For years there had been no accountability, and now there was. The new board, which was trying to sweeten the whole pie rather than fight over the best slices, was working hard. Maybe I should join them? Maybe I could help make a difference, and besides, it represented a good personal challenge: it would be easy for me to stay on the outside and add to the chorus of complaints about the system; what would be much harder would be infiltrating the system and to help fix it from the inside.

As I said, it wasn't an easy decision. Since returning from Australia in 1992, I'd been busy helping a group of kids from the North Kenwood/Oakland neighborhood succeed at getting their educations. That year my sister, Sarah, and I went to work for the Ariel Foundation, which was run by my best friend, a local businessman named John Rogers Jr. John had set up this foundation with the aim of helping local kids get a better education. We'd all been inspired by the work of Eugene Lang, who more than a decade earlier made an impromptu promise to the graduating fifth graders of PS 121 in New York's East Harlem: he would pay the college tuition of any child in that assembly who made it into a four-year university. Thus was born the "I Have a Dream" Foundation, which delivered on its promises. It's grown over the years and has supported more than 18,000 students worldwide.

Sarah, John, and I decided to do a similar thing on the South Side, only on a smaller scale. We would walk across the street from the Sue Duncan Children's Center, go into the Shakespeare School, an elementary school in North Kenwood/Oakland, and offer to take their entire sixth grade under our wing. We did this for a very specific reason: to demonstrate the lesson that we'd learned at Sue's, which was that with love, support, and high expectations, any kid could succeed. We wanted to show that kids who were doing poorly at school because of instability at home, violence in the streets, lack of options in the classroom, and widespread poverty in the community could emerge from that reality and still blossom. Personally, I wanted to prove that if I'd gotten a kid like Calvin Williams a few years earlier, I would have been able to keep his dreams alive. Our promise was the same as Eugene Lang's: between the moment we "adopted" them and the moment they left high school we would support, tutor, and mentor them. If they got into college, then the Ariel Foundation would foot the bill for their postsecondary educations.

The vast majority of them *did* graduate in the summer of 1998. (To put this in perspective, the citywide graduation rate that year was 47 percent—and that was for kids who took five years to get through high school; the four-year rate was a dismal 43 percent.) It had been a tough but intensely gratifying journey for all of us, with more than a few surprises along the way.

The first surprise had nothing to do with these kids' personal lives and everything to do with the school they attended in sixth grade. We went in thinking our students would have a basic level of academic rigor, but in truth there was none. There were no expectations at Shakespeare. Not *low* expectations—*no* expectations. Our sixth graders weren't given assignments; they were given coloring pages, construction paper, safety scissors, and tape. Most teachers at Shakespeare were only trying to keep the kids busy so that they wouldn't fight. A good day wasn't a day when they mastered fractions or learned how a bill gets turned into a law; a good day was a day when no one got hurt. We initially thought that we'd be helping kids with homework, but *there was no homework.* We changed that from the very beginning, giving these kids assignments, tutoring them every day after-school, and putting in long hours in an attempt to bring their academics up to grade level. (Sadly, many of them came to us at a third- or fourth-grade level.)

The second and bigger surprise was that after our first year the city unexpectedly shut down Shakespeare, claiming that the building was in severe disrepair. (After it shut it was used as a location for a prison in the filming of *The Fugitive*. That's about all you need to know: our local elementary school resembled a jail more than it did a school.) We were so appalled that the city would take Shakespeare away from the community that we took our kids and some of the parents down to the CPS board meeting to protest. We had our turn at the mic, and we were heard, but it didn't matter. The board voted that night and the school was doomed. It was hugely disappointing and infuriating. We couldn't understand why they would do something so heartless.

That summer we scrambled to find alternatives for our kids, and we ended up scattering them across the city to all kinds of different schools: public, private, and parochial. It was a logistical inconvenience to drive around the city every day in our white van picking up kids, but before the following year was out we realized that it was the best thing that could have happened. All of our "Dreamers" went from a terrible school with no future to a good or even great one with an established track record. Their work, proficiency, and abilities improved dramatically. They were given homework and expected to do it. Being exposed to a different social framework, with different behavior, had a huge effect on them. By the end of eighth grade, most of our Dreamers were up to grade level and in some cases beyond. One of the lessons learned here—that good schools are infinitely better than bad schools—seems blatantly obvious, but its corollary is somewhat counterintuitive: sometimes closing a school is the best thing that can happen to a group of students. These were lessons I'd come back to time and again later in my career.

If what we encountered at Shakespeare surprised us, what was far less surprising were the personal challenges each of our kids faced day in and day out. John Rogers and my sister and I had grown up nearby, and we'd spent our childhoods with kids a lot like our Dreamers, so we weren't naive. These were kids, nearly all of them black and very poor, whose homes and neighborhoods were more or less devastated. We had one kid whose older brother was gunned down by a rival gang, and for years afterward our student was on the brink of retaliating and murdering his brother's killers, considering suicide, or doing both. We had another whose brother had witnessed a murder and who had to go into witness protection for years afterward. One girl lived in the infamous Robert Taylor housing projects, where I would sometimes go to pick her up or drop her off, and where I would routinely be escorted up and down the stairs to her ninth-floor apartment by the local gang members. We always used the stairs, and never the elevators. These were unreliable and broke down often, and they were a terrible place to get cornered by someone looking to make trouble.

(The projects scared me in ways that other places in Chicago didn't. The first time I went to get her, I sat in my car, waiting for the courage to step out. No one knew me there and no one had heard of Sue Duncan Children's Center. I stood out like a sore thumb, not only with the people who lived there but also with the police. Once, after leaving the Taylor projects, I got pulled over, ordered out of my car, and thrown over the hood. They cuffed me and searched my car for drugs. When they found nothing they finally accepted my story that I was there to help a girl who lived in one of the buildings. It was the first time something like that had happened to me. As I drove off, my wrists still red and hot from the steel, I realized that this is what kids in the community dealt with every single day. I'd gotten off easy. What they regularly went through was much, much worse.)

The list went on. One girl's brother was a drug dealer, her dad had lost a leg to diabetes, and her uncle was an addict who once sold the Christmas ham for drug money. Another boy's parents, both of them decent, hardworking people, fell to crack addiction and abandoned him. He went to live with a local matron named Miss Amelia. Shortly thereafter, Miss Amelia died from ovarian cancer. This student would have then gone into the foster system, and we would have continued to support him, but we knew him so well and loved him so much that one of our volunteer mentors adopted him as her own child. That child is now an adult. Naturally, he's a teacher.

One girl, LaWanda Crayton, loved school. She was whip-smart and hardworking, and always got good grades. Her mom, a nurse, had been a kind, loving, and, most important, *gentle* woman. But then one day a stray bullet struck her in the head and lodged in her brain. She was still loving—she cooked big Southern meals for her girls and made sure they had lunch every day—but her love had toughened, and her gentleness had given way to violence. She began drinking and fought so viciously with LaWanda's stepfather that one or both often ended up in the hospital. I remember going to their house and seeing blood on the walls from all the fights, painted there in brown streaks and splotches, handprints sometimes visible in their contours. LaWanda could never escape the everyday violence underpinning her life—except when she was at school or with us. We were her daily refuge. I can't tell you how many nights I left LaWanda at her house, thinking I might never see her again. Her life was on the line every single day. She told me years later that even though she loved her mom, she and her sister would pray every night for her to die. They wanted to be free that badly.

This is the everyday reality that existed across Chicago's South and West Sides, just as it does now and in countless neighborhoods across the country. It's brutal but it's also banal. Maybe that's the most brutal thing about it—that stories like this are so common.

LaWanda eventually earned her master's degree. In one generation she has broken the cycle of violence that plagued her family. Today she's the mother of two smart and strong daughters, one already in college, the other headed to Sarah Lawrence this fall on a full scholarship to play squash. LaWanda remains in Chicago, working as a project manager for the city, helping kids, many enduring childhoods similar to hers.

After watching our Dreamers graduate, I wanted to do it all over again. I knew Sarah, John, and I could take on another group of sixth graders and change their lives for the better. But I also knew that it wouldn't be enough. Sure, we might help change the lives of another 40 kids, but there were *400,000* children in Chicago Public Schools. The problems facing Chicago's kids and schools were ones of scale. People like Mayor Daley, CEO Vallas, and many others at CPS *were* changing the system. Shouldn't I do the same?

John Rogers and I spoke about it at length, weighing the pros and cons. If I stayed with the Ariel Foundation—which had since opened a new public school, Ariel Community Academy, in the Shakespeare School building—then I could remain nimble and creative. There was no playbook for the kinds of things we did with our Dreamers, and I loved that. On the other hand, moving into a vast bureaucracy would presumably come with a set of constraints and political realities I was not eager to submit to, but that was the trade-off for hoping to put into practice some of the ideas I had about education. Ultimately, John made me an offer: he would give me an open-ended leave of absence. If there was a place for me at CPS, then I would take the job and try it out. If it didn't work, I could return to Ariel.

Now, more than twenty years later, I suppose I'm still on leave. Needless to say, I never did go back.

I managed to consult one more person before joining CPS, and that was Mayor Daley himself. My memory of our meeting is sketchy, but what I recall for certain is that I was nervous and he was as affable and impressive in person as he was in public. I also remember that the exchange was short. I asked him if he thought I should take the job and he said, very much to the point, "Yes." Then he dismissed me and took his next appointment.

I started at CPS in the fall of 1998. For some reason their headquarters were in an old warehouse building at 1819 West Pershing Road. Nowadays when one says, "My office is in an old warehouse," thoughts of start-ups with amenities like foosball and soda machines pop into mind. But this was the late 1990s, and we're talking city government, not Silicon Valley. The place was huge and drafty, taking up multiple floors. Each floor had cubicles and dividers as far as you could see, each with a wooden desk, phone, and chair. There were no computers, no typewriters, and only a handful of copy and fax machines lined up against the far wall. I was shown where to sit, given a yellow legal pad, and told to get to work.

I sat there and thought, *Here I am. In the belly of the beast.* I was young and ready to take on the bureaucracy. I was also determined to test how long my leash would be at CPS. Starting on day one, I called principals, administrators, teachers, and a handful of parents to begin to get a better picture of what the *entire* Chicago school system looked like. In the following days and weeks I got out of headquarters and into the city. I walked hallways, met students, and even shot a few hoops with them. Throughout my life, basketball has served as a great ice-breaker, especially with kids. Before long, I'd travel all over Chicago, even to neighborhoods I'd never heard of before.

Like most cities, Chicago isn't much more than a collection of neighborhoods mashed up against one another. Each neighborhood has its own history and character. Proximity has nothing to do with identity. You can be three blocks from home but feel as though you're in a completely different town, or even a different country, like Poland or Ukraine. The names of some of these neighborhoods can be pretty colorful, while others are more pedestrian. Places such as Back of the Yards, Wrigleyville, the Gap, and the Loop exist alongside places called Kenwood, Hyde Park, New City, Avondale, Bronzeville, and Englewood. Some of these neighborhoods are lily-white and so suburban-looking you wouldn't know you're technically within city limits. Others are nearly all black or Latino, and some of these are so run-down and neglected, they appear to be more ghost towns than towns of living souls. Race matters in Chicago—a lot—and the neighborhoods are generally very segregated, but that doesn't mean there isn't diversity. There are majority-white working-class neighborhoods and majority-black middle- and upper-class neighborhoods; there are even one or two neighborhoods that are racially and economically mixed. There are neighborhoods on the upswing and many others that are struggling.

One thing that sometimes sets Chicago apart from other cities is that people tend not to move around too much. There are Chicagoans who live from cradle to grave in a single community, sometimes within an area of only a dozen or so blocks. I was thirty-four in 1998. I'd gone to school in Boston, traveled all over the country as a college athlete, and been to the other side of the globe as a professional basketball player. But in Chicago I'd barely left my own backyard.

That changed as I explored the CPS system, intent on figuring out how to make it better. I knew black Chicago through basketball, but I didn't know Latino Chicago, white ethnic Chicago, or the new immigrant neighborhoods. My first three projects took me everywhere, and I visited hundreds of schools. Schools like Joan F. Arai Middle School and DeWitt Clinton Elementary School, both on the North West Side, where kids came from all over the globe into these crazy-quilt, melting pot communities that spoke dozens of languages. Some came here to flee war, others to escape desperate poverty, but these children were all united by their parents' hope that they could get a good education in America and live better lives. It was a humbling experience, and the size of the system hit me hard. The spread was huge, spanning all categories. Some of the best schools in Illinois, and even the country, were in Chicago—places like Whitney Young, Walter Payton, and Northside College Prep. These coexisted in the same city, in the same district, with some of the worst—places like Dodge, Terrell, and Williams, all elementary schools on the South and West Sides. Chicago had it all.

As I moved around the city I ran headlong into plenty of lies that permeated the system, all of them propped up and enabled by the bureaucracy. Mayor Daley spoke often and eloquently about the need for cultural change at CPS and what that would mean for Chicago and its children. There was so much to learn. As I listened to Mayor Daley, I began to understand the need for systemic change, and the need to put children first at the most basic policy level. These challenges are the same today as they were back in Chicago in the late '90s.

The hard truth is that, today, our schools *must* improve,

otherwise our country will continue to fall behind our worldwide peers and America's star will fade. I've tried to stay away from numbers so far, but here are a few, all courtesy of the Organisation for Economic Co-operation and Development (OECD), which has thirty-five member nations:

- The United States ranks 31st for three- and four-year-olds in pre-K enrollment.
- For high school fifteen-year-olds, we are tied for 30th in math achievement, which is below the worldwide average; 19th in science, which is at the worldwide average; and 20th in reading, which is also at the average.
- Our college graduation rate of 39 percent ranks 16th, only a single percentage point above the OECD average. To put this in perspective, in 1995 we were first, with a 33 percent graduation rate.
- Using any positive metric, we are top 10 in nothing.

There are many reasons why the United States has lagged in the realm of education, but one of the things holding us back is that sometimes our educational bureaucracy puts kids in the middle or even at the back of the line; on the policy level, they can fall behind teachers, administrators, politicians, and sometimes even the men and women who run the school *buildings*. We as adults love to say that children always come first, but too often that's simply not the case. We either put our interests first, vastly underestimate their potential, or both.

I saw some of this in my very first assignment at CPS. I had to implement a new policy that required high schoolers to complete forty hours of community service before they could graduate. Students could work at a soup kitchen, plant trees, spend a week with Habitat for Humanity, remove graffiti, volunteer at a senior center, paint a mural—we gave them plenty of options so they could choose something that interested them, but they had to choose. This was a new requirement, and it wasn't universally well received. A lot of students complained, "I have to do something *else* to graduate?"

Many Chicago teens came from places where they were the *recipients* of services, not the *providers*. I believed that if they were given responsibilities, then they would embrace them, and that the chance to serve others should be a normal part of a healthy adolescence. This is true for poor kids and wealthy kids. Our Dreamers had these kinds of opportunities, and as they got more and more experience, they were able to do tasks that were more and more complex. It was a progression; it built confidence and a real sense of self-esteem.

On the part of some adults, there was also reluctance to mandate the service requirement. Some thought giving teens more things to do would lower graduation rates—that some kids would choose to drop out rather than do volunteer work for the community. I hoped that wasn't the case, but there was only one way to find out.

We put the program into effect and found these concerns to be completely unfounded. The students quickly discovered their communities didn't just want their help, they *needed* it. It didn't matter if the people of the community was black, brown, white, Latino, Asian, first-generation American-born, mixed, immigrant, rich, poor, or middle-class. Wherever people lived, they liked seeing their young people improve their community, even if the work they were doing was mandatory and only amounted to forty hours per student. In fact, it was so successful, and the students responded so positively, that many students didn't stop at forty hours: they went for one hundred, two hundred, or even five hundred hours of service work over the course of high school. Some students went into thousands of hours.

Nor did it negatively affect graduation rates—quite the contrary. After the service requirement went into effect, graduation rates ticked upward. It was such a simple idea, and it benefited countless people on multiple levels. The program continues to this day, almost twenty years later.

Another lie I encountered was one that the system told parents, children, and principals about Chicago's magnet school programs, which offered students specialized courses of study like math and science or the visual arts. The programs were meant to give students opportunities, and their schools weren't bound to specific geographic areas like neighborhood schools were, but instead accepted kids citywide based on lotteries.

For whatever reason, many of these schools claimed to offer multiple specialty programs all under one roof. Students read about them in a brochure CPS printed each year and handed out across the city detailing programs at both the elementary and high school levels. What many kids found were schools that boasted four, five, or even six specializations, but when they went to visit—or, worse, when they started attending—they discovered the programs didn't exist. It was simple false advertising, and no one seemed to know how it had happened or what the truth was. So my intern and I decided to audit these schools and figure out what they really offered.

We went from school to school and surveyed the principals, some of whom were unaware CPS literature said their school offered programs it didn't actually provide. The principals happily went on record: *Yes, our school does have a robust social studies program, but no, we don't have anything resembling a specialized course of study in the sciences*; or *Yes, we are good with math, but not so great with general humanities, and you can forget about the central office's claim that we teach the performing arts.* In many cases these schools didn't even have teachers to instruct students in the specialties CPS claimed they offered! We were clear that our goal was not to shame or punish these schools, but simply to get them to embrace what they were good at. In short, we wanted truth in advertising. After doing our analysis, presenting our findings, and spending several months reconfiguring schools, the brochure was revised. We were finally able to give an accurate picture of what was available to students citywide.

Another lie at CPS revolved around a group of city employees known as school engineers. You might not think each school required someone with the title "engineer," but in Chicago that was the case. The engineer's primary function was to oversee the building itself, not unlike a ship's engineer. Schools don't embark on journeys in the same way that ships do, but they do need an accredited union member to make sure the building is up to code, safe, warm in winter and cool in summer, and generally in a state of good, school-going repair. They're an essential, if mostly invisible, component to making education work. Which is one reason they had a contract with CPS.

It was that contract on which we ran aground as we floated out a new program spearheaded by Maggie Daley, with whom I worked closely. It was called After School Matters, and, like the service requirement, it targeted high school students. Mrs. Daley's idea was to give poor high school students after-school enrichment options similar to those enjoyed by their wealthier peers. Not only would they be learning something new, they would be forming new friendships, gaining new skills, and learning how to trust others—and, just as important, not be hanging out on the corner with nothing to do.

After School Matters had a basic requirement, which was that schools needed to stay open into the afternoon and evening. But no sooner did we begin talking about these programs than we were told it was impossible to keep schools open after classes ended, which was often as early as 2:30 p.m.

It was a well-known fact that, according to a clause in the engineers' contract, schools could *only* be kept open if an engineer was in the building. Unfortunately, their contract also stated that if a school's engineer stayed past regular school hours, then he or she would get double-time pay. There was no way the CPS budget could accommodate that. As a result, Mrs. Daley's project was a nonstarter.

I despaired over this, but also refused to believe we couldn't find a solution. I couldn't understand why something so technical could be held up to impede improving the lives of kids. I wasn't so much angry at the engineers as I was angry at a system that allowed this to happen in the first place.

To help see our options, I asked CPS's labor and contract lawyer, a gregarious and outgoing guy named Jim Franczek, if we could renegotiate the contract to take that clause out.

"Hell no, Arne," I remember him saying.

"Then what can we do?"

"We can reread it. Maybe they're wrong about when overtime kicks in. Or maybe these guys screwed themselves some other way and we can get them to come around."

"I'm not interested in leverage, Jim. I'm interested in keeping these schools open so kids can use them."

He grunted before hanging up. I very much appreciate what lawyers do, but in that moment I was thankful I'd come to my senses and not gone to law school.

I hoped he'd find something, not just for the kids but also because the whole thing felt personal. I didn't talk about it with Jim or too many other people, but the whole reason my mom's program was in a church all those years was the Shakespeare School couldn't or wouldn't stay open after-school to house the

Sue Duncan Children's Center. It made no sense to her back in the 1960s, and it made no sense to me at the tail end of the 1990s. School buildings are huge physical assets that are chronically underutilized—sometimes for reasons as pointless as the issue we had with the engineers.

A couple days later Jim called back and said, "Well, Arne, they definitely get that double time if they stay late."

"So we have nothing, then?"

He paused before saying, "Oh, no. We have something. Listen to this . . ."

Jim proceeded to tell me the system had it all wrong. He read me the clause, and it couldn't have been clearer. The engineers didn't have to stay in the buildings at all. *Someone official* had to be there, but that person only had to qualify as the "principal's designee."

"It can be anyone," Jim explained. "A principal could designate the engineer, and in that case the engineer would get his extra pay. But it could also be a teacher, a coach, an assistant, or the principal himself. It could even be the janitor or the lunch lady. It could be an unpaid volunteer, or someone running After School Matters!"

That was all it took—for one smart lawyer to take the time to read the actual contract—to discover the truth. This wasn't so much a lie as it was an urban myth that had been passed down and accepted for years. I still have no idea how it got started, but however it happened, the bureaucracy's inertia perpetuated it. And now it was gone—*poof*. All we had to do was tell people they were mistaken and read them what the contract actually said.

After School Matters was not in the clear, though. One more lie stood in its path, and it had to do with the mind-set of certain CPS principals.

One such principal told this lie directly to Mrs. Daley and me, and I'll never forget it. We were at an exploratory meeting in 2000, hosting Mrs. Daley and some administrators to talk about starting After School Matters at a small group of high schools. The engineer problem had been solved, and now we had to convince the schools to come on board.

"This thing isn't going to work," I remember the principal saying. His name was Chester Herberts. Chester was a tough old-school principal with a heart of gold, but he'd seen it all and was very set in his ways. "It's not cool for teens to stay after-school. They don't want to hang out here."

Mrs. Daley listened politely but remained steadfast. "Why don't we give it a shot, Chester? It worked out at Block 37"—this was an apprenticeship program Mrs. Daley had been involved in way back in 1991 and that we were using as a model—"It might fail, but don't you think we should try?"

Chester steeled himself. "With all due respect, Mrs. Daley, if we do this, are you really going to come back out here and stay involved? I doubt it." It was an awkward but honest question, and while I didn't say anything, I appreciated that he had the courage to ask what other principals were surely thinking: *Is the mayor's wife really committed?*

Mrs. Daley had the tact not to make an issue of it, respectfully insisting she *was* in it for the long haul. I tried to be supportive, saying, "For what it's worth, I think this'll work, Chester. I've been to schools just this week where security guards were sweeping kids onto the street after the final bell. Those kids are being pushed out into who knows what."

"Doesn't happen at my school," he said, shaking his head.

"Maybe not, but it happens at schools a lot like yours. It's like they said in the movie *Field of Dreams:* If you build it, they will come. I really think they will. If I'm wrong, then it didn't work and we'll shut it down. No harm in trying, right?"

Chester eventually relented. After School Matters started up not long afterward at his school, and it was an immediate success. With help from local businesses, program providers, dedicated staff, and grants from the Robert Wood Johnson Foundation, After School Matters eventually expanded across the city. It remains to this day, and now serves more than 20,000 teens every year. Going back to the original Block 37 program, more than *200,000* Chicago teens have taken part. They've learned about dance, biology, poetry, journalism, sports management, robotics, graphic design, literature, filmmaking, photography, catering, urban planning, and much more—basically anything an engaged person might find interesting or worthwhile.

Less than a year later I ran into Chester Herberts, who was happy to tell me that he'd been dead wrong—about the kids and Maggie Daley too. She quietly and without fanfare visited high schools repeatedly that year to see how her "baby" was doing, including Chester's school. For his part, Chester had seen hundreds of kids flock to the program, and he now saw how important it was to them. Both he and Mrs. Daley would support the program for years, and Maggie Daley chaired the After School Matters board until her passing in 2011.

I loved Chester's honesty throughout—first when he challenged Mrs. Daley and then when he told me he'd been mistaken about his kids. If we—and, more important, our teens—could win over someone like Chester, it gave me confidence that we could win over anybody.

And to think that none of it might have happened if Jim Franczek hadn't carefully read a contract and pointed out an innocent lie none of us had bothered to check.

"THE NUMBER IS ZERO-POINT-TWO."

Less than a year later, in the summer of 2001, a midlevel no-body who didn't have a secretary would be tapped to replace Paul Vallas as CEO of Chicago Public Schools.

That nobody was me.

This news took CPS and the city by surprise, and while the ultimate decision also surprised me a little, I had an idea it was coming. Specifically, I'd been tipped off at two lunches, each of them with a person whose surname was "Daley." The first was with Maggie, and the second was with the mayor himself.

The lunch with Mrs. Daley took place following an encouraging visit to a school having a lot of success with After School Matters. As we left the building, she touched my arm and asked, in her gentle but insistent voice, "Do you have time for a bite, Arne?"

It was the mayor's wife. Of course I had time.

I got in my Honda and followed her city-issued minivan, eventually stopping in front of a Chicago institution called Italian Village. It had been around since the 1970s and looked the part, with a brown-and-tan exterior, a giant red neon sign, and a small semicircular marquee over the entrance. It always looked to me like a relic from a bygone era, which I suppose it was.

Mrs. Daley and I went in together and the staff jumped to attention. Italian Village was the kind of place that claimed to make everyone feel important, but if you really were important, then they went the extra mile, and there were few, if any, Chicagoans more important than Mrs. Daley. We got the royal treatment, including a quiet table away from other diners and a server dedicated to us.

I can't remember what I ate—probably pizza and a side of spinach—but I do remember the conversation. This was in the early spring. It was cold outside, and Chicago had a couple more snowfalls to go before the weather turned, but there wouldn't be any more blizzards and we'd already had a few warm days. In other words, change was in the air, which was true at CPS too.

For weeks, rumors had been circulating that my boss, Paul Vallas, would be making a run at governor. From the day Mayor Daley appointed him CEO, we'd had no major scandals and not one teachers' strike, which was significant: since 1969, when the first strike occurred, Chicago families had endured more than a dozen teachers' walkouts. Under the leadership of Daley and Vallas, that ended. The relationship with teachers and the unions was still complex, but it was much improved, and during Vallas's tenure CPS had secured two multiyear contracts without any work stoppages. He'd also instituted accountability for bad schools; expanded summer school; opened sixteen charter schools; undertaken a huge capital program to rehabilitate crumbling buildings and infrastructure; and been trying hard to figure out ways to assess and then fix failing schools. Chicago schools had even garnered national attention when they were mentioned in President Clinton's 1998 State of the Union address:

> When we promote a child from grade to grade who hasn't mastered the work, we don't do that child any favors. It is time to end social promotion in America's schools. Last year, in Chicago, they made that decision—not to hold our children back but to lift them up. Chicago stopped social promotion and started mandatory summer school to help students who are behind to catch up. I propose to help other communities follow Chicago's lead. Let's say to them: Stop promoting children who don't learn, and we will give you the tools to make sure they do.

Along with Mayor Daley and the school board, Vallas deservedly got a lot of credit for many of the things that were improving at CPS, as well as all of the things that were going poorly (test scores were notoriously hard to move, and during the end of his tenure had even taken a dip). The upshot was that by 2001 he enjoyed a high and favorable public profile, which in the world of politics translates to opportunity. Hence, he set his sights on the governorship.

At the time of my lunch with Maggie Daley, Vallas was yet to formally resign, but Mayor Daley knew it was likely only a matter of time—meaning Mrs. Daley knew too. At some point, she steered our conversation toward this inevitability. I was completely taken aback when she said, "You know, Arne, I think you would be great as CEO."

I probably choked on my pizza crust as I said, "Wow. That would be—I would love the chance, Mrs. Daley. If that's what the mayor wants."

She didn't respond to that. "Of course, you've only been here for a couple years, so we might have to hire someone in the interim—to keep things going while you get ready. But after that, I don't see why you couldn't take over. I think you would be an excellent fit."

I leaned toward her and said, "First, thank you very much, Mrs. Daley. But with respect, I'm ready now. I've been at Paul's side for a while and I've seen how it works. I get the system. I'm ready for the job."

Her reaction was cool but not dismissive. "It's different when you're in charge, Arne," she gently warned, her hands smoothing the napkin on her lap.

If anyone had a healthy perspective on the responsibility that came with running a behemoth city department, it was Mayor Daley's wife. Naturally the job would be hard on a day-to-day basis: this was Chicago and CPS was a tough beat. But I knew that there would be more and better chances to improve the system as CEO. That was why I'd come to CPS in the first place.

I was getting ahead of myself, though. Mrs. Daley complemented her husband—she was his quieter, warmer, more human side—but she was not the mayor and this wasn't a job offer. It was nothing more than a statement of her support, and I had no idea if it would evolve into something more.

For months it didn't. But then one Saturday morning, after an event the mayor held at a playground opening in Humboldt Park, he stopped me and said, "Hey, Arne, want to go to lunch?"

As with Mrs. Daley, it was impossible to say no.

This time I left my Honda behind and rode in the mayor's car, with a tail following us. It was the first time I'd been in his vehicle, but it wouldn't be the last. We made small talk, and he occasionally stopped to take notes about something he saw outside he didn't like—things like uncollected garbage, giant potholes, or busted street signs. No doubt someone would get an earful on Monday about each of these municipal blemishes.

We kept going east toward the lake and ended up at the Chicago Yacht Club in Monroe Harbor. It was the first and only time I've been there.

As with my lunch with Mrs. Daley, we got a table set off from the others, this time with views of Lake Michigan stretching as far as the eye could see. Almost immediately after ordering, the mayor peppered me with questions: "How would you like to see the system change?" "Where do we need to build new schools?" "What should we do with the findings by the Consortium on School Research?" "What should we do with some of these failing schools we can't seem to turn around?" "How can we recruit more great teachers to work at CPS?" "How can we get graduation rates up?" "How should we deal with budget constraints?" "What about charter schools?" "How can we get to more kids at an earlier age?"

His questions went on and on, but it wasn't a grilling. It was a casual yet in-depth conversation with lots of back-and-forth, and it revealed a side of Mayor Daley I'd never seen. I knew he had encyclopedic knowledge of the city and of the schools, and I knew that when it came to education he was willing to put his neck out further than anybody, but I'd never seen him so real and relaxed. This was Daley the man, not the politician or public figure. All the bluntness and bluster were gone. I liked it.

I answered as many questions as I could. I told him that in extreme cases I thought it was appropriate—even necessary—to close schools that couldn't improve. I told him what had happened to all of our Dreamers after the Shakespeare School closed. I told him we needed to treat good teachers and good schools with more respect and give them more credit and support while at the same time holding all teachers more accountable. I believed then—and I *know* now—that good teachers don't want bad teachers anywhere near the children they care about. There's nothing worse than, say, being a good sixth-grade teacher who has a terrible fifth-grade teacher before them. I told Daley we had to expand after-school opportunities, including tutoring, because that was what would help our students catch up and get ahead. I told him that because we operated under such tight budget constraints, I was all for using more research data, whether it came from the Consortium or from another place doing good work. My point was pretty plain: "Data doesn't tell the whole truth, but it doesn't lie. If we can use the Consortium's data to figure how to spend our money in a smarter way, then we should."

I probably concluded with something like, "Basically, Mr. Mayor, what I'd like us to do is challenge the status quo. We have to do it carefully and respectfully and smartly, but the way things are now isn't close to good enough. Are they better than they were? Yeah. We've done some amazing work. But there are simply too many kids we're still failing."

Mayor Daley listened quietly. Knowing what to say and when—and when not to—is a big part of being a politician. At no point did he offer me Vallas's job or ask if I'd be interested in heading CPS. He never mentioned Vallas's name or any of the political intrigue surrounding him. Also, none of the mayor's questions were framed as *What would* you *do?*—instead they were posited as *What should* we *do?* It was crystal clear he was vetting me, but at no point did the mayor tip his hand. Still, the meeting was a good one. I liked the mayor and I think he liked me. If nothing else, I left the Yacht Club knowing I was in the running for a job I badly wanted. That felt pretty good.

We exited the club together, but Mayor Daley got in his Town Car and I was left waiting for a cab back to my car in Humboldt Park.

I knew I couldn't whisper a word of this to anyone, with the exception of my wife. Mayor Daley prized loyalty. If I ran my mouth and it ended up in the press, then that would be the end of it. If I really wanted a chance at CEO, I'd have to stay quiet.

I was very busy at work, and my wife, Karen, was four months pregnant with our first child, so it wasn't hard. The thought of being CEO was exciting but also nerve-racking, and for several weeks I tried to comprehend the reality of what it would be like to have the job. How would I build a team? What would we prioritize? How could we have the biggest impact on kids' lives?

I'd begin answering those questions soon enough: later that spring the mayor offered me the job, and I enthusiastically accepted.

I could write a whole book about my time at CPS, although I'm not sure how many people would read it. Instead, I'd like to tell you a few stories about the experience, and I'd like to use data as a lens through which to view each story. As I told Mayor Daley, data didn't always give the whole picture, but it could be counted on not to lie.

I started as CEO in July of 2001, determined to split the CPS operations into two camps: one devoted to education and the other to the business of running the nation's third-largest school district. I was most concerned with the education end of the operation, and so my first order of business was hiring a chief education officer who had courage, who believed in kids, and, most important, who would provide the kind of moral leadership I wanted CPS to embody. "Moral leadership" is a phrase that gets bandied around by men and women in suits far too often, but this wasn't some empty quest of mine and I knew who I wanted: the tough-as-nails but vibrant principal of McCosh Elementary School in Woodlawn on the South Side. Her name was Barbara Eason-Watkins, and there was quite possibly no better principal in all of Chicago.

I'd never met Barbara before asking her to be my partner, but in some ways I felt like I already knew her. I certainly knew the type: if my mom had been a principal, then she would have operated exactly like Barbara. Over the course of the previous five or six years she'd turned her elementary school from a low-achieving place with kids who didn't believe in themselves to a high-achieving place with kids who knew they were competing with their suburban peers. Barbara's methods were not always by the book, but they were effective. She championed her good teachers, got test scores to improve, and even invited gang leaders into the school to demand they stop shooting during school hours and create a safe zone around the building. Remarkably, they listened and agreed. (Ironically, Barbara was terrified of mice. If she saw a mouse scurry by, she hopped onto the nearest chair and started yelping.)

She ticked a couple of other boxes too: she headed a regular neighborhood school and not a magnet, and she was an elementary school principal. CPS counted about five hundred elementary schools versus roughly one hundred high schools, serving four times the number of K–8 kids than high schoolers. (A typical Chicago elementary school goes from kindergarten to eighth grade.) This was mostly because there were more grades, but it was also due to the fact that grade schoolers don't drop out. Elementary schools had full grades, whereas it was not uncommon for high schools with freshmen classes of four hundred kids to have senior classes of one hundred or fewer.

Barbara also knew how to improve an elementary school, and this drove right to the heart of one of my mom's greatest lessons: if you can get kids when they're young, then the system has a much better chance of improving their lives.

Another thing I liked about Barbara was that she was a results-oriented person who, like me, believed in numbers and data. She had strong instincts and a great nose for how to achieve educational success, but she didn't run on intuition alone.

Perhaps most important, Barbara had already turned down job offers at the central office multiple times. That was *exactly* the kind of person I wanted to help lead CPS: not a careerist but an educator who put kids above a title or a salary.

She took her time thinking it over and ended up accepting—which came as a great relief, since I had no plan B.

As Barbara and I began our new jobs, it looked as if we might get some outside help too. Congress had recently passed the bipartisan No Child Left Behind Act, and there was every indication that President Bush would sign it into law. (9/11 postponed this signing, but it happened in January of 2002.) Barbara and I were glad to see the feds put an emphasis on making decisions based on the scientific collection of data. I was very happy to see them breaking down students into every conceivable group and subgroup so we could access real numbers for black kids, white kids, Asian kids, Latino kids, special-needs kids, kids living in poverty, and everyone in between. Analysts called this "disaggregating" the data. If we as a nation were going to have a shot at advancing our academic system, then we needed a baseline—we needed to know who was doing well and who wasn't. A very basic example might be a suburban school where 80 percent of students were proficient in math. On the surface, this school appeared to be doing great. But when you broke that data down, you might find 90 percent of the minority and special-needs kids—which represented only a small fraction of the student body—were not proficient at all. The total numbers, or "aggregate," data hid what was really going on, and No Child Left Behind was designed to do the country a huge service by mandating that we look at subgroups of students rather than whole populations. As a nation we had to face the fact that poor, minority, and special-needs kids, as well as kids who were learning English as a second language, were too often getting ignored. Neither Barbara nor I were enthusiastic about the enforcement mechanisms built into No Child Left Behind—it kinds of crises I typically spent time managing. The first crisis that directly involved a child happened on the first day of school in 2001. It was a bright September morning. I had a black chauffeured Town Car of my own by then, a luxury I was still unused to, and I made the rounds to about a dozen schools all over the city to see how things were going. I started early with the mayor at a South Side elementary school, where he rang the opening bell. From there I ran the gamut from poor neighborhood schools on the South and West Sides to high-performing magnet schools on the North Side and closer to the lake. I walked hallways, popped into classrooms, and spoke to principals. I probably shot some hoops too. I'll never forget the exhilarating high I felt that day.

But then, a little before lunch, I got a call that a kid was missing. He was in fourth grade and had gotten on a CPS bus but wasn't in class. I went to his principal to get the lowdown and then I did what I would have done if he were one of my own kids: I told my driver to retrace the bus route and together we searched the neighborhood, looking block by block for a short black boy in a pair of hand-me-down Kobes and a brand-new *Shrek* backpack. We didn't find him. Luckily, he turned up before the final bell, safe and sound. Somehow he'd gotten off the bus at the wrong stop without the driver noticing and found his way to school on his own.

While there was no fallout from this incident—truancies, intentional or not, are a dime a dozen in a large school system—it was an object lesson in crisis management and setting priorities. If a child was missing or in danger, all my instincts and training told me to go out and help that child. But the Chicago school district was so large that I could do that all day, every day, and if I did, it would bog me down. Instead, I had to focus on the bigger picture and on getting wins for the entire system.

One early win came from an unexpected source, a University of Chicago professor named Steven D. Levitt. You may have heard of Steven: he's the research and academic half of the team, with Stephen J. Dubner, that produced the wildly popular *Freakonomics: A Rogue Economist Explores the Hidden Side of Everything*. But since this was 2001, and that book wouldn't come out until 2005, he was nothing more than an obscure number cruncher who lived and worked in Hyde Park.

Steven cold-called me one day and introduced himself as a local economist who'd developed an algorithm that could sort through test data to pinpoint cheating teachers. When I asked what he meant, he explained that by running test results through his computer he could figure out which teachers were changing answers on fill-in bubble sheets in order to make themselves look better. CPS had implemented so-called high-stakes testing in 1996 with the aim of identifying both high-performing schools and schools that weren't meeting minimum standards. Good teachers don't need to cheat, but the worry was that some teachers who knew their students weren't learning might fudge results in order to make it look as if their kids *were* in fact learning. This had always been a concern of ours, but if it was actually happening, we couldn't figure out how to find the teachers involved. Now here was a man whose credentials suggested he could find them, and he was offering to do it for free.

"Have you done this before?" I asked.

"Yes and no. I've run randomly generated results through the algorithm, so I know it works. But I haven't been able to get access to any real-world data."

"So you want ours?"

I thought I heard some resignation in his voice when he replied, "I know it's a big deal, Mr. Duncan, and I know you've just started at CPS. I've asked several other big-city districts for their numbers and each of them has turned me down, so . . ."

I could make a good guess as to why: many superintendents don't want to know about cheating teachers. This isn't quite lying; it's just avoiding the truth. What good would come of it? Publicizing it would cause turmoil with the teachers' unions, principals, local government, and PTAs. If the problem was endemic, then whole bureaucratic swaths would be accused of complacency or worse, and heads would have to roll. If the problem was limited, it would still result in the firing of teachers, which was never pleasant, and the status quo was all about keeping things pleasant.

While I wasn't eager to fire anyone, I did want to understand more about the system I now headed. I also wanted people to know that I planned on doing things differently. Data would help us make the best use of our very limited resources and, I hoped, provide empirical evidence for a priori ideas that Barbara and I—and many others like us at CPS—had about how schools actually worked. For example, I knew in my heart that after-school programs mattered, but could we prove that? Could we prove that getting to kids when they're younger rather than older was the right strategy? Could we show that student achievement at a young age was a good indicator of later success? And what surprises did the numbers hold? What was hidden within them? To turn a popular adage around, what trees were we not seeing because we were too focused on the educational forest? For these reasons, I looked upon Steven's offer as a golden opportunity. If we had bad teachers, then I wanted to know, and I knew that our most essential group of employees would want to know too: *good* teachers.

Finally, I was trying to think ahead. I believed in our kids, and that Barbara and our team could improve academic performance over time. But I didn't want anyone thinking we were cooking the books: CPS had endured its share of scandal, and I wanted none of it. If we could send an early shot across the bow that we were going to have zero tolerance for cheating, it would give us greater credibility for other things we did later on.

"The numbers are all yours," I told him.

We gave Steven a database of test results for every CPS student between third and seventh grade between the years of 1993 and 2000. This amounted to 700,000 sets of results and nearly 100,000,000 individual answers, so he had his work cut out for him.

Steven details how his algorithm works in *Freakonomics* and I encourage you to read it, but the upshot was that about 5 percent of teachers system-wide were changing results in some fashion. Interestingly, in 1996 there was a spike in suspicious test results, indicating that, with the advent of accountability, teachers were suddenly more prone to cheat. Another interesting surprise came in the year-to-year results. Steven shows that one group of kids had averaged a 4.1 on their end-of-year fifth-grade test—meaning they were equivalent to a fourth grader in the first month of school, which was dismally low—and then a 5.8 on their end-of-year sixth-grade test—which was still a full year behind, but which showed an improvement of one year and seven months over the course of sixth grade, which was excellent. The problem was that the following year, at the end of seventh grade, this class dropped to 5.5—three months *below* where they'd been at the end of sixth grade and over *two years* from where they were supposed to be! This indicated that their sixth-grade teacher was not only a likely cheat but was also exceptionally bad at their job.

Just as it had done to Calvin Williams in an earlier era, the system was lying to children and their parents—thousands of them. Imagine a student who might have had the extreme misfortune to get two poor teachers in a row, in sixth and seventh grades. In eighth grade he would be in for a rude awakening, finding himself two, three, or even four years behind grade level. This student would find it nearly impossible to recover. Before the age of fourteen, the child's path through life would be more or less set, and it was not a path lined with roses or opportunity. This was one more example of how the system could not correct itself—how it came up short year after year.

practice of closing terrible schools. I like to think that in Chicago I'll be remembered for things like the 150 community schools we created (community schools are ones that open early and close late, offering services like literacy programs, health clinics, and free meals, in addition to after-school activities not only for kids but for adults in the community as well); or how we tripled the number of advanced placement classes in high school; or how we increased high school graduation rates by 12 percent. Unfortunately, more than anything else, I'll probably be remembered for closing a small handful of low-performing schools.

In that first year Barbara and I looked at all the schools in the system and decided that only three elementary schools warranted closing: Dodge, Williams, and Terrell. This represented one half of 1 percent of the total number of CPS schools, meaning that we weren't being willy-nilly. All three had mostly black students and were on the South or West Side, and all had been failing their students for years. On average, only 13 percent of students at these schools were at or above grade level in reading, and since 1996 each school had shown a consistent lack of improvement. For this reason and a few others, Barbara and I determined that it was time to shut them down and start anew.

Even though CPS had the right to do so, no elementary school had been closed for poor performance since Mayor Daley gained control back in 1995. Barbara and I consulted with a team of people within CPS and the mayor's office, all of whom had been sworn to secrecy. If word got out that we were closing these schools, then there would be a media firestorm that would be hard to work around. We decided to inform teachers, principals, and parents at the same time in April 2002. We knew the unions would be upset—the union president, Deborah Lynch, would say that she felt "betrayed" by these closings—as would their members, the parents, and, most important, the children.

We sent teams to each school to deliver the tough news on a Tuesday and mailed an announcement on Wednesday to be safe. I heard that some kids left school that day with tears rolling down their cheeks. Parents were irate; teachers were in shock. We were accused of lots of things, including trying to empty the neighborhood of black families to pave the way for gentrification; of intentional neglect; and of all-around heartlessness. It was perhaps the first public action we took that gave those aligned against the idea of closing and fixing schools a rallying point. The general critique was *They want to fix schools? Then fix this one!*

I knew how terrible it felt from my experience with the Shakespeare School. And while it's fine to say *Fix this school,* that takes time. These three schools had been on probation for years with nothing to show for it. They'd graduated thousands of kids who were not prepared for high school, which all but eliminated college as a possibility. These children had one shot at an education, and we had failed them.

We knew that there were other schools within walking distance that were doing four times better—not 4 percent better, but *four times* better. Dodge, Terrell, and Williams each got additional funding because of their on-probation status, funding that these other successful and nearby schools did not get. The other schools were literally doing more with less, getting dramatically better results for kids with identical backgrounds. We couldn't accept this. Our plan was to close the three schools, reopen them with new principals and new teachers, and see if we could replicate the success of other schools in the neighborhood.

To explain why this was happening, I planned to go to each school and address an assembly of parents. I remember the one at Williams in particular. I stood in front of the room with a mic, my sleeves rolled up. The anger was palpable, and I didn't fault them for it. I tried to explain that closing the school was not an indictment of the teachers or the principal or the parents themselves. I tried to explain that it was our fault this was happening and that this was an attempt to change things for the better.

This was perhaps a poor way to start my conversation. They came right at me: "If it's not the fault of the teachers, then why fire them?" "If it's not the fault of Williams Elementary, then why close it?" Some of the parents in that room were alumni of Williams and had positive memories of going there. These were neighborhoods that had next to nothing in the way of community resources, and here we were shutting down one of the most important ones. How could we do that in good conscience?

I remember one woman standing up and saying point-blank, "Mr. Duncan, you're just doing this because you're a racist."

I took a moment before answering. "You can think whatever you want about me, ma'am. But if you'll give me a moment, I'd like to share some things with you and everyone in this room."

"Please, share away."

"Which grade is your child in?"

"My child? I got one in the third grade and one in seventh."

"All right, let's talk about the third grader. I think there are about seventy third graders at Williams. Does that sound right?"

"I guess. Yeah."

"Do you know how many third graders are reading where they're supposed to be?"

"They all moved up last year, so most of them? My seventh grader's been here the whole time and she never got left back or anything."

"Six."

"What?"

"Six third graders are proficient readers. None are advanced. Everyone else is at second-grade level or lower."

She shook her head. Her eyes widened. "*Six* kids can read?"

"That's right. Maybe yours is one of those six. I hope he—he?"

"She."

"I hope she is." I looked from her face to the other faces in the room. "How many parents here have third graders?"

About fifteen hands went up.

"Do any of you know if your kids can read at grade level? If you know they can't, would you be willing to leave your hands up? If you know they can, how do you feel about the fact that over ninety percent of their friends are having trouble? Anyone?"

The hands went down slowly and no one answered. "Listen . . . your kids can't afford to wait for this school to get better." I paced back and forth a little before continuing. "We have a number that measures how much a class learns each year. A one-point-zero means they learned exactly one year of material. A one-point-five means they learned one and a half years of material. Care to guess what that number is for the kids here, on average?"

"A little less than one?" the mother said. She was in the front row and she'd sat back down, her hands in her lap.

"The number is zero-point-two. *Zero-point-two.* There are roughly one hundred and eighty days in a school year; it takes your kids that long to learn what it takes a child just blocks away thirty-six days to learn. It's taking your kids *five years* to learn what many other kids learn in one year. That's not fair. Your children are falling further and further behind the longer they're here. We're hurting your children, and for that, I'm so sorry. That has to stop, and it's what we're trying to change now."

I could feel the anger and tension in the room dissipate in that moment. "Like I said, you're free to call me a racist, but I'm not one, ma'am. If I were a racist, then I would leave this school exactly as it is. That's not what I want. They're children; I believe in them as much as you do. They can't wait for things to improve any longer."

By the end of the meeting, the entire dynamic in the room

had changed. Parents approached me individually and in small groups. They wanted to talk about their kids and they wanted to hear about our plans. They didn't trust us yet—we would have to earn that—but they felt we were sincere in our commitment and they were willing to give us a chance with their most precious resource: their children.

To start to build that trust, we took some of these parents to nearby schools and showed them what was possible. It was eye-opening. Dodge, Terrell, and Williams had not presented the data to the parents. Instead, they tried to craft a counter-narrative that the school was not as bad as it actually was. In the case of Williams, I'd attended an event just one month earlier celebrating the school's achievement in science. The problem was that while some students did deserve the accolades, the school itself remained miserable. That was what we attempted to show this group of parents.

CPS closed all three schools in June of 2002, and in the fall of 2003 they were reopened under new leadership. Each improved markedly and continued to improve for several years. In time, some of the angriest parents from these first three closures became some of our staunchest allies. They partnered with us and helped us communicate with other parents at other schools that we closed in the following years. (I'd note that the ratio of school openings to school closings during my time at CPS was about four-to-one, and that we only closed about two dozen schools over seven years.) It was a huge lesson for me: the parents who were the angriest were simply fighting the hardest for their children. They weren't defending the status quo; they were demanding the best for their children. That's a great thing. Rather than running away from angry parents, I learned to go right to them.

From them, I learned always to run *to* the fire.

THE
CONSORTIUM

Earlier in these pages I cryptically mentioned the "Consortium on School Research." This was not some cabal of education-obsessed partisans but rather a group of serious researchers based at the University of Chicago.

The Consortium has been around since 1990. Created on the heels of the reform movement that began in Chicago in the 1980s, its original mission was to be an objective observer of Chicago's public schools, not necessarily for the benefit of the system but to function as a tool that would serve the public interest. It was funded almost entirely by grants and foundations, and only rarely accepted small amounts of money from CPS, usually to help pay for printing reports. The Consortium was unique because it held up a near-magical, independent mirror to the system as a whole. It was a truth teller, and the truth coming back was not always flattering.

At the time, the Consortium was led by a soft-spoken researcher named John Easton. I'd been acquainted with John for a few years and had nothing but the highest opinion of him. Tall and reed-thin, with wavy hair that he combed straight back, he was the perfect embodiment of a professorial researcher, but he was much more. He regularly left his office and went into the schools, and he knew the system and its people intimately. In fact, when he called to offer his congratulations on my promotion back in 2001, I clearly remember him saying, "Arne, I know who you should go after for chief education officer." When I asked him who that was, he said, "Barbara Eason-Watkins. You'd be a fool not to hire her." He was unwilling to risk my not knowing who Barbara was, which I greatly appreciated.

"Don't worry, John. I'm way ahead of you. Between you and me, I'm not considering anyone else." He was glad to hear it.

During my seven and a half years as CEO of CPS, the Consortium provided regular reports and insights into Chicago's schools. It could take them years to gather data on things like test results and graduation rates, but since they weren't in the business of hoarding information, they gave us annual updates. The theory was we didn't need to have the whole picture to start addressing problems.

So, every August, before the new school year began, I'd

assemble about 125 of our top leaders to discuss plans and review the previous year's results. As a part of those assemblies, we would meet at a lecture hall at the University of Chicago's business school for a presentation by John. One year in the mid-2000s I remember walking in on a high. There was a real sense of momentum, schools were getting better, attendance was up, dropouts were down, and the percentage of students meeting standards on the state tests was rising year after year.

John stood at the front of the room, a clicker in hand, and talked us through a series of PowerPoint slides on a topic that was hugely important to us: whether there was a correlation between test scores in elementary and middle school and the scores that high school juniors got on the ACT. Scores on the ACT, like the SAT, are decent predictors of college readiness, so the higher the score, the better.

John began by explaining that too many of our kids weren't scoring above a 20 on the ACT. In case you don't know, a 20 was below the national average by a few points, but it was high enough to get into some colleges; at smaller Illinois institutions and a few historically black colleges, it represented a typical score for new students. If we wanted more Chicago kids to go to college, which we did, then it followed that we needed more of them to hit at least 20 on their ACT. Since this was a modest score, we felt this was achievable, but moving the needle would take time: fewer than half of Chicago's students got a 17 or higher. The average score was just above 17, and only one in four scored 20 or higher. (Each year we'd have a couple hundred kids score above 30, with four or five getting a perfect 36.)

We knew all of this as we sat listening to John. We also knew that about three-quarters of Chicago's high school juniors weren't ready for basic college-level work. The raw numbers were even worse than the percentages, since by junior year so many kids had already dropped out of school. This meant that those who were still in the system, as unprepared as they were, represented the best the city had to offer. Kids who had dropped out weren't captured by the stats, but you could bet that the vast majority of them were not college ready.

The dropout and college readiness issue was endemic. Just to make up an example, let's say there were 100 freshmen at Chicago High in a given year. Based on city averages, when this class hit senior year, its size would have would have dropped to around 50 students—the other kids had simply stopped attending school. Of those 50, roughly 13 were ready for college. Further, of those 13, about 6 would one day graduate with a college degree. And the truly depressing number? If you took 100 freshmen who were *only* black or Latino, only *3* would graduate from college by their mid-twenties.

Our desire to understand and be cognizant of these kinds of numbers was why we worked with the Consortium: to get hit in the face with cold water and then look deeper into the data to figure out how to best go about changing things.

The mystery we were trying to unravel on that day was why,

before these kids were struggling in high school, they were doing just fine in elementary and middle school. All of the eighth graders had taken the Illinois Standards Achievement Test, or ISAT, and most had done relatively well. The scores on this test could fall anywhere between 120 and 410, and a score of 246 was the lowest possible score for "Meets Standards," which is what some other states call "Proficient." So many of our kids were hitting this number that we assumed they'd be fine once they got to high school.

That was a *very wrong* assumption.

What was happening? Were these kids suffering epic summer slides between eighth and ninth grades? Was high school such a hard social, educational, and logistical transition that these kids were falling off the achievement cliff like a horde of lemmings? Or, what was more likely, were they getting hurt in some way we couldn't discern?

What lie were we telling ourselves that kept these kids from succeeding?

I pondered this as John worked through his slides, not gaining any insights or getting any wiser. But then he stopped on a chart that took me a minute to understand.

"On the Y-axis we have the percent of kids who score a 20 or more on the ACT," John explained, "And on the X-axis are ISAT math scores. The dotted vertical lines are the cut scores for 'Academic Warning,' 'Below Standards,' 'Meets Standards,' and 'Exceeds Standards.'" He drew his laser pointer over the bars that went from 0 percent on the left side to close to 100 percent on

Only students who exceed standards on their eighth-grade ISAT math tests have at least a 62 percent chance of scoring 20 on their ACT.

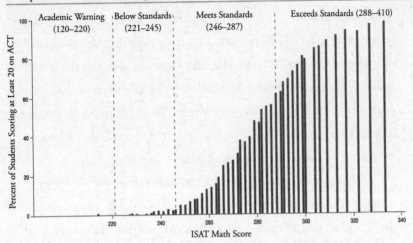

Source: Easton, J. Q., Ponisciak, S., and Luppescu, S. (2008). *From high school to the future: The pathway to 20.* Chicago: University of Chicago Consortium on Chicago School Research.

Note: This sample includes 40,099 students who took the ACT as eleventh graders in 2005, 2006, and 2007, and who also had eighth-grade ISAT scores three years earlier.

the right side. This was completely expected. A kid who was in academic warning, on the left side, had virtually no chance of getting a 20 on the ACT; a kid who scored highest on the ISAT, on the right side, was virtually guaranteed a 20 or higher.

"Here's where we were surprised, though," John said. The red laser circled a cluster of very short bars in the middle of the graph. "These kids were being told they were proficient. The reasonable assumption would be that that trajectory would continue, and that these kids would have a good shot at getting close to 20 on the ACT as a junior. But in fact, we've found that a kid right in the middle of 'Meets Standards' has only a one-in-five chance of doing that." My throat went dry as he moved the laser's dot to the right. "These kids here scored in the middle of the 'Exceeds Standards' distribution, and they have about a four-in-five chance of getting a 20. In other words, kids who think they're doing *just fine* at the end of middle school are wrong. They're not ready for high school—not even close. Our conclusion is that the state's standards are way, way too low."

What this meant was that these categories had to slide one slot to the right. Kids who were "Below Standards" were actually in "Academic Warning," those in "Meets Standards" were really "Below Standards," and those in "Exceeds Standards" were in "Meets Standards." I'm not sure what we would call the kids in "Academic Warning," but odds were that they would not be successful later on in school or in life.

The dry feeling in my throat dropped into my stomach and I immediately felt sick. A lot of data is boring because it's either hard to understand or simply confirms what you already believe. But this crystal-clear new information was shocking. Every one of us in that room and across the CPS system—including parents, teachers, and principals—thought our middle schoolers were being well prepared for success. The truth was they weren't.

CPS was powerless to revise Illinois standards; only the state government in Springfield could do that. But what we could do was try as hard as we could to get as many middle schoolers into the "Exceeds Standards" column as possible. We needed to move tens of thousands of kids to the right on that graph, because that was the only way to ensure that they would be truly prepared for college. Anything less than that would set them up for failure.

Now, you might wonder why the "Meets Standards" category was so far off, and initially we wondered the same thing, but it didn't take long for us to realize what had happened. No Child Left Behind tried to make schools better by penalizing them if they didn't improve. Test scores *had* to go up over a period of several years—the law demanded 100 percent proficiency nationwide by 2014—and if they didn't, then federal funds could be withheld from the states. Again, it was all sticks.

What would have to happen to meet these No Child Left Behind mandates? Test scores would have to go up. You can improve test scores by doubling down on instruction, by caring more, by tutoring kids, by doing away with the "soft bigotry of low expectations," as President Bush so eloquently and accurately described it to the nation. But raising scores this way involves *hard work*, and No Child Left Behind made no mention of *how* states could or should go about bringing up test scores. Perhaps the feds were afraid to step on toes: a national education law was already a big deal for a Republican president, and more federal "overreach" stipulating how things should be done made it a nonstarter. Or perhaps the president and Congress naively assumed that states would do the hard work, because that was the right thing to do.

There are other ways to improve test scores, of course. One is by making the tests easier, but this also involves a lot of work. A far simpler way that involves practically no work is by lowering cut scores. Overall, a state could define success downward.

This is exactly what the state of Illinois—and nearly two dozen other states as well—did in reaction to No Child Left Behind. In order to abide by the law of the land with a minimum of effort, Springfield took the easy way out and quietly weakened statewide standards.

This was what we confronted that day with John and his PowerPoint presentation. Our goal was never just to improve test scores; it was to get kids ready for college. We thought that if we did the former, then it would lead to the latter. The truth was that while test scores were going up, thousands of kids who were being told they were proficient really weren't. They weren't on a path for success in college; they weren't even on a path for success in high school. The state was lying to us, and in turn we were lying to thousands of children and families. That had to stop.

Lowering standards does nothing to help students and everything to help adults—politicians, district superintendents like myself, and teachers' unions. It also does nothing to help teachers who are working hard to help their kids. The lower standards rewarded people who thrived on the status quo and—no surprise—did nothing to help kids break out of poverty. They also did nothing to improve the lot of Illinois long-term, but the politicians didn't seem to care about that. It wasn't so much that they had moved the goalposts—those appeared to be in the same place—as they had secretly rewritten the rules. A touchdown would no longer be worth six points; it would be worth three, but the scoreboard wouldn't tell you that. The whole thing was disgusting.

Much of my remaining time at CPS was devoted to doing everything possible to get more of our students to score at least a 20 on their ACTs. This included moving as many of our kids into the "Exceeds Standards" category as possible. It also included a huge push to keep kids engaged once they got to high school. Remember the attrition rate at our hypothetical Chicago high school? If a kid dropped out, then that was it. He or she would not get a second chance. So how could we cut down on dropouts? And how could we do that immediately?

To help achieve this, the Consortium unearthed some really powerful and somewhat unexpected predictors for high school graduation, all which concerned freshmen. If a student got a single F in her freshman year, then she had a 60 percent chance of graduating; if she got two Fs, it was 44 percent; three Fs, 31 percent; four Fs, 22 percent; and so on. Meanwhile, her friend who got zero Fs in freshman year had an *83 percent* graduation rate. This correlation may seem obvious, but it was revealing. If we could get more kids to pass their freshman classes, then more kids would graduate, pure and simple. If more kids made it to the end of high school, more kids would take the ACT. If more kids scored a 20 on the ACT, more kids would be better prepared for college. If more kids applied to college and submitted their Free Application for Federal Student Aid (FAFSA), then more kids actually would *go* to college. (Our district was 85 percent below the poverty line, and nearly 100 percent weren't higher than middle-class, meaning that almost every single kid in a Chicago public school was eligible for some kind of financial aid.)

The question we then asked was: Why does a freshman get an F? Because he's not ready for high school, or because he doesn't like a teacher, or because math is first period, among other reasons. What do we do? We intervene. Since we didn't have enough money to hire an army of social workers, everyone working at a high school was assigned a group of six or seven freshmen to stay on top of. We met kids where they were, not to coddle them but to make a deal with them: we'll help you out with this problem but you have to commit. We showed them that we were in this together, and that it was for their benefit.

We also figured out that kids who didn't come to the first day of school in September were disproportionately prone to getting Fs later in the year. So what did we do? We tracked first-day truancies, went to their homes, and asked them to come to school. I and many others in CPS went to these kids' houses and apartments and talked with them very honestly, told them to their faces that if they didn't come, then they had no shot at graduation, and if that happened, then what did they think their life would look like? Most of these kids didn't have to look farther than the guys on their street corner to know that their lives might be much harder if they didn't make it through high school. This tactic didn't always work, but it edged things forward, and that was important.

We also learned that a lot of kids didn't fill out college applications because they didn't know how to, and no one in their family had the knowledge, time, or capacity to help them. We stayed on them later in high school and made sure they did. The same was true of financial aid forms. Failure to fill out the FAFSA, which seems routine to some of us, translated to millions of kids nationwide not going to college. In Chicago, we brought them in with their families and helped them fill it out.

Finally, if they needed help in their studies or showed a desire to do better on the ACT, we offered them free after-school tutoring. Makes sense, right? We thought so, but the federal government did not.

In 2005, I went to Washington, DC, to meet with Secretary of Education Margaret Spellings. Earlier that year we'd been ordered by the US Department of Education to shut down our CPS tutoring program, which I thought was insane. Mayor Daley agreed. We continued tutoring, daring the feds to enforce the law and end our program. Our sin was that we had the audacity to use federal money to pay our own teachers and local nonprofits to tutor kids after-school. For reasons I still don't understand, this use of local resources was forbidden by No Child Left Behind. Nationwide, there was $2.5 billion in federal funds that could be used for tutoring, but this money had to be used to hire outside companies, and since the passage of the law a host of private organizations had sprung up and rushed into the breach. I have no ideological problem with hiring private companies to provide a service or even run a school, but it has to be done well and there has to be accountability. In Chicago, we had a set amount of federal money and tens of thousands of kids who needed help. We had to stretch every dollar as far as we could to reach the maximum number of students who wanted to stay after-school and improve their skills.

Using data, I was able to show Secretary Spellings that we could tutor our kids for $400 per student per year, versus $1,800 per student per year for the private providers. Furthermore, the results we got were better than the ones the private instructors got, in part because our tutors already knew our kids and were able to meet them where they were.

We applied for a waiver, arguing we could help more than four times as many kids without any change in funding. I talked about the magnitude of the need and how committed our students were to improving. If the feds forced us to go with the private providers, then we'd have to tell tens of thousands of teens that they couldn't get the help they wanted. It made no sense. Thankfully, Secretary Spellings agreed. She gave Chicago the second No Child Left Behind waiver nationwide (the first had gone to Virginia), and the first to a large city school district. Almost immediately, Los Angeles asked for a similar waiver, and over the following years the dominoes began to fall. The law, while well-intentioned, was horribly constructed, and it seemed inevitable that it would eventually fail.

It was not a total loser, though. As I wrote earlier, what it got right was that it broke students into different groups and sub-groups so we could see how one set of students was doing in comparison to another; resources could be allocated and adjustments made accordingly. This was important, and it would have a huge effect on how we dealt with data when I was in DC. But what it got wrong was that the force compelling change came in the form of sanctions. It was a punitive model, as if the Department of Education were interested only in rapping the bad school or district on the back of the hand with a ruler, taking away funds and resources, and not at all interested in rewarding the good school or district that served as a model. Which schools and districts were improving the fastest? How were they doing that? What could we learn from them? None of that was in the equation.

Worst of all, No Child Left Behind was loose on goals and tight on means. I can't tell you how many times I've said this phrase over the years. What I mean by it is that the law wanted scores to rise across the country, but because the country's education system was completely decentralized, the goals were all over the place and many states dumbed down their standards, just as Illinois had done. At the same time, the means—the sanctions, the rules, the fixes—were way too rigid. Our fight to get the waiver demonstrated that perfectly.

We made a lot of progress in Chicago when I was at CPS. As I write, "Chicago's growth rate is higher than ninety-six percent of all school districts in the United States," according to a recent Stanford University study. It also points out that "each successive CPS class is outperforming the class that came before and improving at a rate far above the national average." But all this does not mean that the work is finished—and it certainly wasn't finished as I left CPS. The lies persisted. The biggest remained the poor statewide standards that did nothing to prepare kids for the de facto nationwide standards as measured and dictated by the ACT or the SAT. The federal government was attempting to lift all boats, but you literally could not compare one state to another. The tide was empirically rising in places like Massachusetts and Tennessee, but it only appeared to rise in places like Illinois, Texas, and Oklahoma. In an ideal world, I thought more states should have higher and more closely aligned standards. Wouldn't it be nice if what a kid learned in El Paso was equivalent to what a kid learned in Nashville or Boston? Wouldn't it also be nice if we could bring states together to aspire toward higher standards, rather than punishing them for failing to achieve results on their own? Wouldn't these be good ways to make the country stronger, more resilient, and better prepared to compete in the global economy?

I and many others thought that basic knowledge should be transferable all over the country, from Anchorage to Key Largo. We thought that all of this should be transparent so that we could know how any given kid was doing at any given moment.

But in truth, none of this was the case. No Child Left Behind was failing. More change was needed.

On December 14, 2008, as the financial world fell apart and school districts faced impending budget cuts that would be devastating, I got a call from a guy I'd never spoken to before. I can't recall his name, but he was part of President-elect Obama's transition team and he sounded like a young person fresh off the campaign trail. Barack and I had been friends for a number of years. I'd met him through my close friend Craig Robinson, whose sister, Michelle, was then dating Barack. We played pickup basketball games together at the University of Chicago's Henry Crown Field House, where, believe it or not, he would sometimes square off against my mom. She was nearly thirty years older than he was and he was a good shot, but she was a defensive hound who never shied from contact, a fact that Barack regularly reminded me of.

Professionally, we'd worked together on education issues when he was both a state and US senator, occasionally visiting schools together. One of those visits was to Dodge Elementary, one of the first schools we'd closed at CPS. He was intrigued as to why the Dodge students were doing so much better since it had reopened and wanted to find out more for himself. We visited the school one morning, went into classrooms, talked to kids, teachers, parents, and the principal. He asked question after question: *How is this possible? What's different?* I vividly remember one teacher who'd been there before Dodge had closed and was then rehired saying to him, "Before, our students were referred to as 'those kids, those kids, those kids.' They're not 'those kids.' They're *our* kids." This resonated with him so deeply that he wrote about it in his book, *The Audacity of Hope.* He was so moved by what was going on at Dodge that I eventually had to leave him there to go to my next school visit. I have no idea how long he stayed.

Since his election victory, he and I had sat down a couple of times to talk seriously and at length about education. We found that we were largely on the same page, but, like Mayor Daley before him, Barack never came out and offered me the job. In the following weeks there were plenty of rumors as to who he'd pick for secretary of education, and my name came up along with a handful of others, including Michael Bennet, my good friend and the superintendent of Denver Public Schools in Colorado.

I purposely stayed as far away from any politicking that took place and continued to serve as CEO of CPS. I knew that Barack would vet each of his candidates thoroughly and make the right choice, whomever he ended up choosing. If you can believe it, I had no indication as to what that decision would be when the young man from the transition team called and said, "Mr. Duncan, if it's possible the president-elect would like to announce his nominee for secretary of education at Dodge Academy in a couple days. He said it would make a perfect backdrop. Is there any way you can talk to the principal and make that happen?" I told him of course I could and that I thought it was a great idea. He thanked me and quickly hung up. I was so preoccupied with whatever I was working on at the time, it wasn't until a few minutes later that I called him back and asked, "By the way, who is it?"

The man's voice cracked as he replied, "Hasn't anyone told you?"

"Told me what?"

There was a pause before he choked out the words. "Well, um—let me be the first to congratulate you! You're going to be the next secretary of education."

I tried to absorb the news as quickly as I could and managed to say "Thank you."

"You should probably get to the Dodge school early. The

"WE NEED THE CARROT."

Armed with dozens of black briefing binders, I immediately moved to Washington to prepare for my Senate confirmation hearing and then my new job. My wife, Karen, went about the business of selling our home in Chicago and finding a new one in the DC area. (The best advice I got from the outgoing secretary, Margaret Spellings, was to move somewhere close to work *and* the airport. We ended up in Arlington, Virginia, where the public schools also happened to be pretty good.) Making the sacrifices that so many government spouses make, Karen also dealt with our kids—a six-year-old daughter and four-year-old son—pulling them out of their Chicago schools and settling them in new ones in Arlington. The kids were young enough not to be too bothered by the move, but they had their concerns. My daughter wanted to make sure we could bring the cat, and my son wanted to know whether "people speak English there." Karen and I answered yes to both, so they were good to go.

As far as schools went, our daughter was easy. She went into the local public school's first grade right in the middle of the year. Our son was trickier. Karen tried to get him into a Montessori preschool but, owing to his "lack of Montessori experience," he was denied a spot. We never told them why we'd come to town or what my job title was, and we moved on. It took a few weeks but he ended up in a Jewish Day School that worked out great.

Although we were dealing with dislocation, Karen and I were acutely aware of our good fortune. While we had no savings to speak of and couldn't afford to keep our home in Chicago—I promise that no one gets rich by serving as CEO of CPS or as secretary of education in DC—we could afford to move to a community with good public schools, and Karen could afford not to work while she figured all this stuff out. These were luxuries that most American families didn't have. People were largely at the mercy of their zip code—and often their race and socioeconomic standing as well. That was a fact I'd seen up close in Chicago over and over and over again, going all the way back to my mom's center. But I wasn't in Chicago anymore. I was in DC. I wasn't contending with 600 schools in a single district, but with 100,000 schools across 14,000 districts. Nor was I dealing only with the city of Chicago or the state of Illinois. I was now dealing with every American city, town, and county across all fifty states.

And then there was the money.

Imagine how the average American might answer the following: "In terms of total spending, including federal, state, and local governments, what are the three most expensive programs in the United States?" They'd probably answer, "Defense, social security, and . . . something." Or: "Defense, health care, and I don't know what else." Or maybe: "Health care, pensions, and defense." How many would place education—and here I mean K–12 *and* higher-education expenses—in the top three? Not many. And yet, consistently for years and years, total spending on education nearly always outpaces the nation's defense budget. As I said, this includes money spent on higher education and some research dollars, but even when you pull these out of the equation, we still spend about $650 billion a year on K–12 education, or about $12,000 per student. It's an astronomical sum of money that goes out every year like clockwork, paying teachers, principals, janitors, tutors, superintendents, and coaches, among many others; and covering expenses like pencils, Smart Boards, tablets, Internet service, capital programs, and, yes, basketballs and backboards too.

Furthermore, this $650 billion represents only the money spent on *public* education. If you added the reams of money Americans spend on private and parochial schooling, after-school programs, tutoring, and all the money raised by PTAs, bake sales, and school auctions, you'd have a total education sum that probably exceeds $1 trillion every single year, easily eclipsing our bloated defense budget.

Yet, for all we spend, when we compare our educational outcomes to other industrialized nations, we're middling or worse. You might be shocked to learn that 68 percent of community college students, 40 percent of open-access four-year college students, and 20 percent of four-year college students take at least one high school–level class because they're not ready for college coursework. Simple stuff, like basic algebra or subject-verb agreement, needs to be "remediated" for these students because they're unprepared. Even some kids who graduate with honors (like Calvin Williams) or with GPAs above 4.0 aren't ready—because the system lied to them. Most perversely for these students, many of whom find their college dreams compromised and, in too many cases, completely dashed, they need to spend college tuition to get up to speed. Nationwide, according to one study, we spend *$7 billion* a year on remedial classes at community colleges that earn students zero college credits.

Like many in government and education, I knew that these trends couldn't continue if the United States wanted to retain any measure of competitiveness across the entire economy, from the arts to biomedical research to manufacturing to services and everything in between. They would have to change if we were going to educate ourselves to a better future.

One reason people don't realize how much money is spent

on education is that the federal government accounts for only 10 to 15 percent of our $650 billion in annual education spending; the rest is covered by states and municipalities. The federal portion pays for aid that the Department of Education grants to the states, as well as the cost of running the Department. In the context of the federal budget, this amount is middle-of-the-pack—about $65 billion a year, give or take. For comparison, in 2008 the Department of Agriculture got $91.9 billion, the Department of Housing and Urban Development got $49.7 billion, and the State Department got a meager $17.7 billion.

From my perspective, though, $65 billion was a huge amount of taxpayer money. It dwarfed the $5 billion we spent each year at CPS.

What this money represented to me was *scale*, and it fit right alongside the career path I'd been following. I'd started with individual students at my mom's center; branched out by adopting 40 sixth graders in the "I Have a Dream" program; took on about 400 students through my involvement with the Ariel Community Academy; was lucky enough to help 400,000 students when I ran CPS; and was now atop a federal agency whose purview counted more than 50 million students nationwide. The numbers were staggering. Whenever I took a moment to reflect on them, or whenever I realized I was an actual cabinet secretary in a presidential administration, I was overcome with the feeling that my life had taken an amazing but surreal turn.

What was more surreal, however, and far more important than my feelings, was the economic wildfire raging across the entire country. When we came into office in January 2009, the financial crisis was completely uncontained. In the last four months of 2008 alone, 1.9 million jobs had vanished. Historically, the education job market is pretty stable, but if things continued this way, then teachers wouldn't be immune. We had to protect them.

Amid this cloud of bad news there were some glimmers of light, though. It looked as if Congress and the president would be able to pass a stimulus package to bolster the economy. The total package would be worth $787 billion, and since the election we'd been talking about setting aside some of that money for education. A lot of it, actually: $100 billion. If the stimulus package passed, it would give Education the opportunity to help the entire system from Hawaii to Maine. Armed with an *extra* $100 billion, the term "scale" (and my sense of surreality) took on a whole new meaning.

When I first spoke to the career staff at the Department, I acknowledged that while we'd probably get a windfall of additional resources, we couldn't let them go to our head. We were stewards. The country was suffering and we were about to get this huge gift from the taxpayers, and we could never forget that that's what it was. We were not entitled to this money; we were *charged* with it. Our goals shouldn't be modest, but how we did the work mattered and we couldn't waste so much as a nickel. I wanted the Department to aim high but be humble. I also hoped we could do things a little differently. I tried to drive this home when, during that first speech, I insisted that no one call me "Mr. Secretary" or "sir" or anything like that. "I'm Arne. Just Arne. I might be the only person in this building with a security detail following me everywhere—which will take a while to get used to—but that doesn't mean you can't come to me at any time. Also, I've heard there's a tradition where if the secretary gets on the elevator, then everyone else has to get off. I hope that wasn't true in the past, but if it was, then, as of today, it's over. I'd like for us to ride together."

From my first day in the building we got right to work. One of my team's biggest priorities in those early days was to figure out what we'd do with the stimulus money. The original plan was to use about 85 percent to stop the bleeding at school districts nationwide. It would be granted to the states to retain teachers, principals, and staff. The other 15 percent would be put to a different use. With this money we hoped to incentivize states to enact reforms that would improve student learning. Unlike with No Child Left Behind, which used sticks to punish states for not meeting goals, we would only use carrots. This program even had a nifty name: Race to the Top.

A week after the inauguration, on a clear January day, I went to meet with the president in the Oval Office for the first time. Amid meetings on the war in Iraq, the reeling auto industry, and health care, he'd carved out thirty minutes to discuss the education provisions of the stimulus package. The bill would be going to the Hill within days and we needed him to sign off on it. Accompanying me were two advisors: Jon Schnur and Heather Higginbottom. Jon helped conceive the broad strokes of Race to the Top, and Heather, who'd worked as an aide to Senator John Kerry, knew the ins and outs of Washington. Both were borderline obsessive when it came to education reform.

With the president was his senior advisor, David Axelrod, and his famously profane chief of staff, Rahm Emanuel. They were Chicagoans and I knew both pretty well, especially Axe.

It was easy to see some of the risks of doing Race to the Top. First, it challenged some sacred cows on the left: namely, that the teachers' unions were loath to cede any power when it came to deciding how to pay, train, or evaluate teachers. And second, Race to the Top was a competition that would produce winners and losers among the states. What if only blue states won? What if Illinois was a first-round winner? Cynics and opportunists on the right would contend that our so-called contest was just window dressing for a tainted political process designed to hand out favors. Some would argue it would be much more equitable if we doled out the money to all fifty states, even if that meant a single state would get a lot less than if it had "won" the Race.

I understood all of these concerns, but I didn't buy them. I was confident the president felt similarly. In early July 2008, he'd given a speech at a meeting of the country's largest labor union, the National Education Association (NEA). He was there to accept the teachers' union's endorsement, but that didn't mean he was intent on rolling over for them—quite the contrary. At one point he said, "Under my plan, districts will be able to design programs to give educators who serve . . . as mentors to new teachers the salary increases they've earned. They'll be able to reward those who teach underserved areas or take on added responsibility. As teachers learn new skills or serve their students better or if they consistently excel in the classroom, that work can be valued and rewarded as well."

He was saying, *Hey, if you're a really good teacher and it's borne out by results, or if you help other teachers, or if you choose to work in a rough neighborhood helping poor kids, then I want you to get a raise.* That sounds logical, doesn't it? Merit-based, professional, even capitalistic. Not at all controversial.

For some of the teachers there—not all, but more than you might expect—these words were heresy, and candidate Obama was treated to a round of boos. To his credit, he didn't back off his position.

It's worth taking a moment to unpack this a little. There are two teachers' unions in the United States: the NEA and the American Federation of Teachers (AFT). The NEA is the oldest and largest labor union in the country, and put together the NEA and AFT counted more members (about 4 million in 2008) than the country's second and third largest unions, the Service Employees International Union and the American Federation of State, County and Municipal Employees combined. Like much of organized labor, the NEA and AFT are staunchly Democratic. Obama was making a huge gamble by touching NEA and AFT third rails like merit-based pay at that July 2008 meeting. The race for president was very much undecided then, and here he was risking the backlash of a significant part of his base. But Barack knew that the old ways weren't helping adults or kids, and if that meant exposing some lies in the service of truth, then so be it.

Fast-forward to the early days of his administration, and we wondered: Would Race to the Top succeed in pushing some of the education reforms that the unions opposed? Could the politics from both the left and the right be overcome? I was less sure about the political calculus of the Race, but I was nearly positive the incentives would work. I'd seen similar incentives work in a Chicago pilot program designed in partnership with the union that encouraged teacher peer evaluations. Done right, I hoped the Race might move half the states toward the reforms we favored, especially higher academic standards.

Axelrod was more circumspect. He was sure that Obama's adversaries on the right, who were still in the early days of getting organized, would use Race to the Top as a cudgel against him, claiming it was a political program and nothing more. I insisted that it wouldn't be that by any stretch—that it would be completely transparent and absolutely fair. It didn't matter if a kid was in the reddest state or the bluest: if his state was willing to help him, then we would support that.

Emanuel shared this view. He was convinced we could get Democratic congressional votes supporting Race to the Top even if there was union pushback. Since this was happening against the backdrop of the financial meltdown, it fit perfectly into his much-publicized mantra of "You never want to let a serious crisis go to waste."

The president agreed. "Let's do it," he said.

Over the course of the next week we wrangled with the appropriations committees in Congress, but it was a done deal. The amount we could use for the Race was ultimately reduced to $4.35 billion, but when the American Recovery and Reinvestment Act was signed on February 17, 2009, a lot of money was made available for us to distribute to the states. The vast majority of the $100 billion allowed states to avert disaster, continue to give college students financial assistance, and also continue to support poorer K–12 schools. This money helped save or create about 400,000 jobs nationwide. It represented an unprecedented investment in the American education system, and said to the American people that education was important and that we would not allow it to crumble or worsen. We got right to work.

While huge to you or me, or even to a large city district like Chicago's, $4.35 billion *divided over four years* is less than 0.17 percent of $650 billion. As a reminder, this last number is the total amount the country spends at the federal, state, and local levels combined on K–12 public education each year. Were we being naive to expect we could change *anything* for this paltry sum? We wanted wholesale changes: higher academic standards, better use of data, a way to deal with failing schools, and teacher evaluation based in part on their ability to help their students learn. If we could have waved a magic wand to make just these changes, then they would ripple through the system, affecting countless other things. They might, over time, also change how much teachers get paid, which I have long advocated should be significantly increased.

When considering how paltry $4.35 billion is in the world of American education, it's important to remember what a figure like $650 billion means. Not what it does but what it means. Sums that high mean there are countless people who get paid. Not only teachers, but testing companies, facilities contractors, IT professionals, coaches, nurses, superintendents, bus drivers, and so on. What figures like this do to large systems is ossify them. They pack them with vested interests that are resistant to change and absolutely beholden to the status quo. If we could wave that magic wand again, I wouldn't decrease the amount of money that's put into the system—in fact, I would double it—but I *would* change who gets paid and why. That's scary stuff. Real people with families and years of hard work are on the other end of that $650 billion, and I don't blame those people for wanting to keep things as they are. The main problem is that the constituency that gets paid nothing, and which is at the center of the entire enterprise, is getting shortchanged. That constituency is our kids. Not your kid. Not my kid. *Our* kids—all of them.

These numbers are so high, and therefore meaningless, that

an analogy is in order. Let's say you make $50,000 a year. Let's also say you're a devoted smoker and hate to exercise. You have some healthier habits—you're a vegetarian and get eight hours of sleep every night—but you're forty now and you need to make some changes. Your employer, who not only likes you but also has an interest in your good health, wants you to make these changes. So she offers some money as an incentive. In exchange, you will commit to quitting smoking and joining a gym and using it. If you fail at these over time, then your boss will intervene with support, but if you consistently fail, then you might lose your job as well as any of the incentive cash.

"Okay," you say after thinking it over. "I'm in."

"Great."

"How much money am I going to get to do all this?"

"Oh, one second. Here."

She hands you a check. It's signed and ready to go. The amount is for $90. "I think you're missing a zero or two."

"Nope."

"Do I get it every year at least?"

"Yep."

"Great."

"But only for four years. After that, nothing."

"Oh. Okay," you say, thinking it over. "All right. Let's do it." Then you take the check.

Or would you take it? You make $50,000 a year, you're single, you have no kids. Just you. You know you should quit smoking and start exercising, but is $90 a year for just four years enough to make you?

Is it?

That was what we faced. We would need a lot of luck and we would have to design and run a top-notch competition to leverage $4.35 billion into massive change. Or, rather, the person we hired to design and run it would have to make it top-notch. By May of 2009 I knew exactly who I wanted: a brilliant and dedicated woman out in California named Joanne Weiss.

Joanne worked for a nonprofit called NewSchools Venture Fund, based in Silicon Valley. This was a nonprofit "venture philanthropy" firm that did all kinds of work surrounding education reform, concentrating on the charter school market, teachers and school leaders, and education technology. It got most of its funding from venture capitalists and tech CEOs who thought they could bring their model of "disruption" to the world of education. The investors—who contributed tax-deductible donations instead of pure investment dollars—hoped for social returns, not financial ones. NewSchools took the money it gathered to support other nonprofits doing great work in education reform. If these ideas worked, then NewSchools' investors would earn pride and prestige. They would get to feel like they were making America a better place, and while that's not hard currency, I'd argue it's worth way more than money.

I'd met Joanne several times at events around the country, and after being announced as secretary of education I invited her to Chicago for a meeting. I told her a little about Race to the Top and asked if she might be interested in helping. She said she would be much more than interested.

It took a few months to get my legs under me at the Department, so I couldn't give her a real interview until May 2009. We flew her out to DC, where we met for about thirty minutes at the conference table in my gigantic office. The office was still new to me and felt way too big; it had an American flag on a pedestal taller than me, tasteful couches, a view of the National Air and Space Museum, and gray wall-to-wall carpeting. It also had a dark wood desk the size of a boat. I never used it, opting to spread my briefing binders and papers across the rectangular conference table. It wasn't just that I was more comfortable there; it was that I didn't want a huge hunk of wood separating me from whoever was in my office. From the moment I walked into the building I knew that we were on the clock, and I wanted all of us to operate as a team. Huge wooden desks undercut that spirit.

I was confident Joanne would share these sensibilities. Not only was she supersmart, she was apolitical and fair-minded, and it helped that she came from the intersection of the private sector and nonprofit worlds. We needed experts from all sides if we were going to make this work. Mostly I knew she cared about kids more than grown-ups. The question I'd heard her ask over and over was, "How do we help kids learn better?"

After her interview she asked if she could have the run of the building for a few hours. "It's fine if I can't spend the day with you, Arne, but I'd like to talk to some of the career people here, if that's all right." I said of course and took five or ten minutes to lead her downstairs before cutting her loose. As we parted ways, I hoped she would take the job.

To my relief, she did. From the moment of her hiring, Joanne dove headfirst into crafting the Race.

Much has been written about the workings of Race to the Top, and while I want to avoid getting too far down in the weeds, some basics still need to be covered.

Right from the beginning I need to admit that Race to the Top's greatest failure concerned communication. In the midst of so much rapid change, we proved to be terrible at explaining the Race's goals and methods to teachers, and even worse at explaining them to students and their parents. We could have done a much better job, and spent a little more money, helping states explain and publicize what they were attempting and what the goals were.

At the most basic level, the goal was to get as many American kids as possible ready for college and careers. This could lead to more fulfilling lives and also help make America successful in the twenty-first century. Many states were already undertaking the work of education reform—we called them the "laboratories for innovation"—and all we wanted to do as federal employees of the Department of Education was help the states amplify and spread their successes. The states were reacting to the fact that their educational systems were not keeping pace with the rapid rate of change taking place around the globe. Quite simply, we needed to upgrade some of the knowledge and skills that kids learned and how they went about doing this.

But what *is* education reform? I like Joanne's definition: "Our schools were beautifully designed to meet exactly their intended purpose, which was to prepare the bulk of kids for assembly-line work in factories while also picking a small number of kids to be the elite that managed those factory workers. This is a completely outmoded way of thinking about education. At the highest level we need to change the way we think about what schools prepare kids to do and how they go about doing that. We need to *re*form education."

We don't need rote knowledge anymore: we have the Internet and Wikipedia for that. What we need are kids who can learn anything and continue to be able to learn anything for the rest of their lives. We need kids who can think, not just recall. We need kids who are comfortable solving problems in a group, working together, supporting and challenging each other, and bringing out the best thinking in everyone. That's what education reform is after: figuring out ways to better equip our children with skills and habits that will make them successful for the rest of their lives.

What are some of the tools we use to hone these skills? Here we need some more basic definitions. We can use standards, curriculum, and assessments (aka tests). These things are constantly confused and conflated, but they are distinct. So: *standards* define what a kid needs to know and be able to do; *curriculum* is the material the teacher uses to teach those standards to that child; and *assessments* are used to measure whether this student knows and can do these things at the end of the year. Seems simple, right?

But consider this: If the standards are upgraded, then the curriculum must become more rigorous. The teachers use this to prepare their students for new tests, which will be both different and more challenging than previous ones. Right away you can see how standards, curriculum, and assessments are distinct yet bonded together. If a group of vested interests is reluctant to change just one of these things, then it can easily use this close interrelationship to stoke people's fears. For example, if one group is opposed to a new curriculum but not new testing or new standards—and if the testing is what is giving students and parents anxiety—then the group opposed to the curriculum can use the anxiety against the testing to call the curriculum into question. This is exactly the kind of thing that would happen, and it came from folks on both the right and the left.

On the subject of tests, it's also important to note the distinction between proficiency and growth. Not everyone understands this, including the current secretary of education. Raw scores are important, but what we're really after is growth. A teacher who starts with a class that's on average three years behind, and who teaches these kids so well that, by the end of the year, they are only one year behind is better than a teacher who starts the year with a class at grade level and ends with that class at grade level.

The first teacher, even though none of her children are proficient, is more effective—her kids made two years of gains—while the other teacher, who's doing a fine job, made only one. This first teacher is a master at work, even if on an absolute basis the numbers showed that all of her kids "failed."

I recently saw a comic strip at a graduate teaching course at Relay Graduate School of Education in Newark that perfectly illustrated the distinction between teaching and learning. In it, a little boy says to his friend, "I just taught my dog how to whistle." The friend looks at the dog, who is not whistling, and asks, "Well, why isn't he whistling?" The boy explains, "I said I *taught* him, I didn't say he *learned* how to do it!"

In other words, the goal of great teaching is not to teach but to have kids learn.

To get kids to learn better, we needed higher standards, new assessments, and brand-new curricula. If we didn't get these, then we'd continue to produce legions of students who would need to take remedial classes in college. We couldn't hurt our kids anymore. Unlike with No Child Left Behind, whose laser focus on proficiency resulted in lower standards and kids who were less prepared for college, we wanted high standards even if they came at the perception of an initial loss of proficiency. We were happy to pay this price in order to stop lying to our kids and their families about what it was they should know and be able to do. We could accept these initial "losses" because, in fact, they would reflect the truth, and from there we would be able to grow.

This is where tests came in: the fairest and most objective way to tell if kids are growing and learning is by tracking their test results over time. We wanted to use these results to help figure out if a teacher was in fact helping his kids learn. In education wonk-ese, this is what's termed "tying teacher evaluation to student learning." It was a big one, because in states like California and Wisconsin, among a few others, it was actually *illegal* for school districts to even look at test scores to help determine if a teacher was doing a good job or not. These laws came at the behest of teachers' unions, which generally resisted evaluations of their members' performance. When I learned about these laws, I was shocked.

What was the lie at the center of these laws? Was it that test scores didn't matter? Was it that teachers couldn't be judged by tests or evaluations, even though their students were? Was it that good teaching was immeasurable? Or was it that some teachers— pointing at poverty, violence, physical abuse, hunger, addiction, or any other societal challenge—preferred to claim that they couldn't help the students who most desperately needed help? *Yeah, maybe that was it. Poverty's destiny, so what's the point?*

The point was to stop telling this lie. This was the same lie that had been told to our Dreamers in Chicago back in the 1990s, and it's the same lie we exposed when we adopted them and showed them they were worthy of a real education, that they mattered, that they were intelligent and capable. It's the same lie my mom exposed over and over and over as she and her team helped hundreds of kids break the cycle of desperate poverty. She used to say, "We all start life illiterate, without knowledge, without skills. Any of us can learn. We just need consistent behavior and no violence. Care for the children. Care for the parents. Be honest. Be open. It works."

This work is hard, but it is absolutely worth it. The children who attended my mother's program proved, year after year and decade after decade, that poverty *was* not and *is* not destiny.

In order to participate in the Race, and with no guarantee of getting any money, states like California and Wisconsin would have to strike down these laws that severed teacher evaluation from their students' test scores. This was the only ironclad requirement of the competition. If a state couldn't do away with these laws, then it could not participate. And guess what? Each and every state that had these laws did exactly that, and in record time.

In a perfect world, as the states rolled out their new standards, we would want tons of training and teacher development, but these would also be up to the individual states to put in place. In fact, *all* of it would be up to the individual states: they were the only governing bodies that had constitutional authority over this component of education policy. Encouraging the states to act on their own was the only way the Department of Education could legally go about getting the kind of change we craved, but it was also the only logical way to do it. We couldn't wrap our arms around 14,000 school districts, but we could wrap our arms around fifty states. As the Race started, the governors of those states became our partners. I wanted each governor to become the best education governor his or her state had ever seen. I talked with every single one, Republican and Democrat, every chance I could get. I still count many as friends.

The basics of the Race were simple but comprehensive. Each state prepared a proposal and provided lots of documentation showing how it would help more kids learn the kinds of things they needed to know for a successful life in the twenty-first century. We gave states points for how well their proposals met the competition's criteria, and the states with the highest point totals would be named the winners. A big component of these criteria was adopting higher, and shared, standards.

We pushed for standards to be shared between at least two states for a few reasons. One was that knowledge is knowledge. When you've grown up and are done with school, no employer is going to ask if you know the Indiana state standards or the Washington state standards; they're just going to ask what you know. Two was that sharing standards would motivate states to work together and learn from each other. Three was that schools would need lots of new materials to support them in implementing standards—curriculum, assessments, teacher development, and so on. We figured that if the best people in the country were focused on designing the best materials to support new standards, then that improvement in quality would benefit everyone.

The application process was intense. It involved governors, state education chiefs, district superintendents, teachers, union reps, nonprofits, community organizations, and business leaders. Each state submitted its application, which was read by a team of five peer reviewers. These were not federal employees but experts contracted to do the reviews. They were paid, but not that much—in the end I doubt the reviewers made much more than $10 per hour—but they were not in it for the money. Each reviewer underwent a thorough screening process to ensure there were no conflicts of interest, and no two review teams were the same. Points were awarded for different reforms: a total of 70 points for the "Standards and Assessments" section, 138 points for "Great Teachers and Leaders," 50 points for "Turning Around the Lowest-Achieving Schools," and so on—for a possible total of 500 points. The reviewers submitted their scores, discussed the applications, then revised and resubmitted the scores. A group of finalists was announced. These were invited to Washington to give presentations on their applications. Up until these meetings, the reviewers remained anonymous to the states, so there was no opportunity to influence them in any way. The presentation had to be given by actual state officials and the people who would carry out the reforms—not by consultants—to make sure the states deeply understood and were committed to their plans. These meetings were the reviewers' final chance to see through any shenanigans, and in the interest of transparency, each of the meetings was videotaped.

Immediately afterward, the reviewers submitted their scores, which were added up and averaged. This was the final tally. I was then handed a sheet of numbers, ranked first to last, with no names. Initially, looking at the numbers, we had no idea which states had won; we did it this way so no one could accuse us of playing politics. We looked down the list and decided where to put the cut score. Every state above that line won, and every state below it lost. After the winners were announced, we would send the states their first batch of money, which was based on how many kids they had in their school districts and not on whether one state scored higher than another. We gave ourselves some flexibility, retaining the right to decide the number of winners per round, but we promised to hold at least two rounds and announce winners until we ran out of money. That was it.

As I said, I often spoke to governors throughout my time at the Department of Education, and this was no different during the Race. As I got to know more of them, I was pleasantly surprised to learn that many, and from both parties, were desperate for the federal government to set these kinds of aspirational goals for the states and the country. I remember one in particular, a Republican from a red state, saying, "Arne, we need the carrot." Having been in similar shoes at CPS in Chicago, I agreed. Yet the question remained: Would the carrots work? Would they cut through the lie that this kind of reform couldn't be done because it was too challenging, because the interests aligned against reform were too entrenched and powerful? Would we wade too far into treacherous political waters? There was only one way to find out. The Race began in earnest on July 25, 2009, and we would announce our first winners on March 25, 2010.

Until that time, I had a country to visit and a department to run. The truth was that I barely knew America. If we were going to change America's schools and help America's kids, then I wanted to see and meet as many of both as I possibly could.

ONE BLUE,
ONE RED

Whenever my staff and I traveled, we always flew on commercial flights and always coach. This was another good way to see the country and meet people—except in this case I was meeting fellow travelers: businesspeople, families, folks going on vacation. I had countless armrest conversations that went something like this:

"What do you do?"

"I work for the federal government. What about you?"

"I'm in logistics. Headed to Memphis for a couple nights."

"Good barbecue in Memphis."

"You're telling me. You travel a lot?"

"All the time."

"What do you do for the government?"

"I work in education." I hardly ever revealed that I was the secretary of education. Most of these conversations were casual, and over by the time the plane was wheels up. Occasionally my job title did come out, though, and whenever that happened, the person next to me would twist in their seat and stare.

"You mean you're *the* secretary of education?"

"That's me," I said. "Arne. Nice to meet you." Education secretaries enjoy a high level of name nonrecognition. That's not a complaint.

At that point we'd exchange pleasantries and I'd submit to a light grilling. I regarded it as another part of the job of public servant. I thought it was good to show that I wasn't that different from any other busy American, and that a lot of people who worked in Washington didn't live in the DC bubble.

If the conversation went on for a while, two questions were inevitable. The first was, "What are you doing in coach? Shouldn't you be up there?" They would jerk their chin toward the front of the plane. "You're pretty tall, too."

"Tell me about it," I said, refolding my knees. I'm six foot five in shoes. "We only fly coach. The travel department usually gets me an aisle, though."

"No private government jet, then?"

"As far as I know, the only cabinet members with their own planes are the secretaries of state, defense, and transportation. Believe it or not, my job doesn't have a lot of perks."

The second inevitable question, and always uttered in a

conspiratorial whisper, was, "Does that mean the Secret Service is on this flight too?"

To which I'd always have to say, "I'm sorry, but I can't talk about that."

The only times I didn't fly commercial were when I was going somewhere with the president or vice president, meaning I flew on Air Force One or Two, which was always a thrill and something I never got used to.

But, man, did we rack up the miles over the years. We went everywhere. Starting in 2009 and continuing every year afterward, my staff organized back-to-school tours so I could get into the less-traveled corners of the country. These excursions were eye-opening. We chartered a bus, which was important: I didn't want to fly to Phoenix or Portland, Maine, and only see the schools there; I wanted to go to public schools that had never been visited by a secretary of education, not just to demonstrate that we were working for all Americans, but also to further my own education. Bar none, these trips were the best way for me to learn more about how schools work all around the country.

So we went to places like Columbus, New Mexico; McDowell County, West Virginia; and Carrollton, Georgia. We went to Worcester, Massachusetts, and inner-city districts like Baltimore, Maryland. We went to schools on Native American reservations and remote schools like the one (and there was only one) at Hooper Bay, Alaska. Each of these places, and countless others I visited, had a story to tell.

In Columbus, I visited the bilingual elementary school on the outskirts of town—where we were greeted by a mariachi band! Surrounded by red and brown desert scrubland, Columbus was nearer to El Paso, Texas, than to any major New Mexican city, and it was also only a few miles from an official crossing into Mexico. On the other side of that border was a Mexican settlement named Puerto Palomas de Villa, or just Palomas to the men, women, and children who lived there.

Many of those children crossed the border every morning before sunrise to go to school in Columbus. Owing to federal and state laws that allowed women, regardless of nationality, to deliver babies at the nearest hospital, which was in the county seat in nearby Deming, New Mexico, these kids had been born in the United States and therefore were American citizens. For the most part their parents were Mexican, but they'd decided to risk living in a Chihuahua border village, which are notoriously unsafe because of the drug cartels, so their American kids could attend American schools.

Every morning dozens of kids would leave their homes— some without running water, electricity, or toilets—and line up to go through the border-crossing process. They showed laminated copies of their birth certificates and handed over their backpacks for inspection. Once through, they would board yellow-and-black school buses and get taken to school. At Columbus Elementary, where three-quarters of the kids lived in Mexico, they got a great American education. The teachers, bus drivers, and principal at this school were remarkable. This was different. They put in extra hours every day to give these unique American students a shot at a better life.

Aside from their living conditions and the rigmarole of crossing into the United States every day, most of these kids were learning English for the first time. Some were barely literate in Spanish and had never seen a pencil before. Some had to be taught how to flush a toilet. Their parents, who were rarely allowed into the United States, were practically nonexistent at the school, but they were engaged in ways I'd never seen before. They couldn't easily attend performances or come to parent-teacher conferences, so they improvised and did these over Skype. In Palomas, parents would head to a local restaurant with a generous owner to watch their children sing and dance, or talk to their teachers about progress in math and science. The arrangement was heartbreaking, inspiring, and genius all at once.

Of course, there's plenty of controversy in an arrangement like this, especially in the current political climate that vilifies immigrants, undocumented people, and Mexicans in particular. But on the local level none of this mattered: the community was unified around helping these kids. For me, this was symbolic of so many issues, and an example of how the noise and drama that fuels Washington was so far divorced from real life in communities across the country. As complicated as it appeared, this was the American Dream in action. Many of these young citizens would eventually live full-time in the United States. They might go on to serve in our armed forces, or go to college, or go into the workforce; each would have the chance to become a productive, tax-paying citizen. New Mexico and this minuscule town of about 2,000 people had the decency to pay forward the education of these kids, knowing it wasn't just the right thing to do but it would also be a good investment over time.

After spending a day at the school, I made an impromptu decision and rode with the kids back to the border. I sat in one of those brown bench chairs toward the back of the school bus, my legs jammed into the seat in front of me, next to two fifth-grade girls. For them, the trip was routine. For me, it was a brief but extraordinary journey between two worlds. The girls—all the kids on the bus—were easygoing, bubbly, and talkative. Most everyone spoke in Spanish. I couldn't help but feel nervous, though, worried about their safety on the other side. The girls I sat with—one of whom showed me a poster she'd worked on for a social studies project—were about the same age as my daughter. As we chatted I wondered whether my wife and I would have had the courage that these kids' parents possessed: Would we have allowed our children to make this journey every day? The trip was routine, but the border and Palomas were dangerous places. The drug trade flourished here. Would I have been willing to take this kind of risk? I wasn't sure.

I'm ashamed to say I can't speak Spanish—I took German for ten years and never used it—but at one point I asked the girls what it was like to go back and forth every day. One of them said, "We're used to it now. But it makes visiting friends in the US a little weird."

"No sleepovers, then?"

"My parents let me go sometimes," one girl said, with barely a hint of a Mexican accent. "But none of my Columbus friends have ever slept at my place! Someday, maybe," she said, and shrugged.

Shrugging was a pretty apt gesture for these kids' approach to their here-and-there existence. The ride from one world to another took less than fifteen minutes. When we reached our destination, the bus turned into a dusty parking lot near the Customs and Border Protection station and came to a stop. The driver pulled a lever and the doors wheezed open. The kids stood all at once, chatting loudly, and filed out. A few thumbed phones as they put in calls to parents. Each kid said good-bye to the driver, who smiled and knew all of them by name.

As I jumped down the stairs I realized I'd never been to a US-Mexico land crossing. There were uniformed agents in dark ball caps and bulletproof vests, some of them armed with assault rifles, milling near the station and around their four-wheel-drive vehicles. They were probably a little put off by the fact that I was a cabinet secretary making an unscheduled visit to their remote outpost, but I greeted them and gave them a Department of Education coin as an act of goodwill. I got a quick tour. The station was flanked on both sides by an imposing fence of vertical metal columns stretching to the east and west over barren hills as far as I could see. Tumbleweeds blew across the ground here and there. It was like something out of a movie.

Columbus, New Mexico, has a unique distinction that's worth noting and which I learned of while touring the school: it was the last place in the lower forty-eight to be attacked by a foreign military force. In 1916, the Mexican revolutionary Pancho Villa took part of his Division of the North and raided the town in search of supplies. The American 13th Cavalry Regiment, which was stationed in Columbus, repelled them and pursued them into Mexico, but both sides took casualties. About fifteen American civilian lives were also lost in the fighting.

Even with the ugly tensions built into some of our current attitudes toward Mexico and immigration, I saw these kids as a fitting coda to that history. I'm pretty sure the history of the Southwest is less black-and-white—or American and Mexican— as some might have it. Certainly a bureaucrat from DC is unable to comprehend this history in the same ways that locals do, regardless of which side of that high steel fence they hailed from. There were no more invading military forces on this border, but on that day—and every day afterward—a parade of children would peacefully cross back and forth from one side to the other, all in pursuit of a better life. Is there anything more American than that?

I stood in a parking lot where our shared bloody history had once played out and said good-bye to the girls I rode with as well as two dozen other kids. The district superintendent and both of our staffs had made the trip too, which probably put the kids on their best behavior, but it didn't matter to me. If you set aside the circumstances, it was like an end-of-the-school-day scene you'd witness anywhere in America. Which made it all the more striking to watch these children, some as young as five, cross to their homes in Mexico.

The trip home was much less onerous for these children than the one into the United States. They just walked across the border without anyone giving them a second look, least of all the American agents guarding against illegal crossings and drugs. I watched as these kids disappeared, some of them holding hands, others laughing, others looking serious. Some would go home on their own; some would get picked up by parents or relatives. I'm sure they would be asked the usual questions: "How was your day?" "How are your friends?" "Did you learn anything new?" There would be dinner, homework, and bedtime. And the next day these families would get up before sunrise and do it all over again.

On another back-to-school tour I saw a different but no less striking scene in Carrollton, Georgia. This town of about 25,000 was in a semirural area west of Atlanta. It was full of hardworking, religious, blue-collar Americans, and it was mostly white but also about 13 percent black and 6 percent Latino. Regardless of race, it was a poor place: the median household income was below the state average, even if you discounted Metro Atlanta and its wealthier exurbs. Like many communities across the country, the Great Recession had hit Carrollton hard.

The school we visited was part of a program called 12 for Life. This was a public-private partnership that helped high school kids who were at the extreme end of the at-risk spectrum. Most were white, and every student I met faced serious challenges. I met a seventeen-year-old who'd repeated the ninth grade four times. I met a girl whose parents were both in prison for drug dealing. I met another who had a child at fifteen. Some kids were homeless, living out of their cars or just outdoors. Except for the color of their skin, these kids weren't unlike many of the kids I grew up around in Chicago, with one other exception. These Georgia teens were part of a cohort I'd never met in force: if they made it, then many of them would be the first in their family to graduate—*from high school.*

I'd known plenty of black and Latino kids on the South and West Sides whose parents had not made it out of high school, but I'd never seen kids like these collected in one place as they were in Carrollton. Their school was atypical for this reason but also for one other: it was housed in a manufacturing and distribution facility belonging to a company called Southwire.

This private company, worth about $6 billion, made cabling and electrical wire and shipped it all over the world; it was committed not just to developing its business but also its community. Starting in 2007, an executive named Mike Wiggins partnered with the local school board, and together they started the 12 for Life program. The meaning of the name was simple: completing twelve years of education would give graduates a better shot at life.

Trying to find ways to increase high school graduation rates (the county's dropout rate in 2007 was 35 percent), and also to help their business grow, Southwire and the district landed on a novel idea: take troubled kids who'd been shuffled around and lied to by the system and put them to work, train them to be leaders, and give them an education. The ground floor of the school, which was renovated by Southwire at a cost of more than $3 million, was a fully functioning distribution facility. Above the factory floor were brand-new classrooms. Students, who would not be allowed to go to class if they didn't show up for work, would do four-hour shifts downstairs and then go to school upstairs. Southwire had more than a dozen business locations across the United States and in Mexico, and many of its workers were highly skilled, but the company also needed unskilled workers. Teenagers who needed a second (or third, or fourth) chance in life fit the bill perfectly.

These were kids who'd never been given any responsibilities and who had rarely been held accountable for anything. They were kids who'd been told straight up that they were worthless. At this school they were told the opposite: they had value, and they could develop it, and they could be successful people. Not just workers—*people*. These students, not unlike the Dreamers we adopted back in Chicago, were implored not to give up and were given the support they needed to get through the program.

Working with the county school board, which provided teachers, a principal, and transportation, Southwire delivered. These teens learned real lessons at school and earned a real living at the factory. They made better money there than they would have at the local McDonald's or Chick-fil-A, and they learned actual life skills. They were given duties and rewarded for demonstrating leadership. The arrangement also benefited Southwire, which, during the year of my visit, was looking at pretax profits north of $1 million on their 12 for Life investment. That was not an accident; that was intentional. Southwire's goal was to have this partnership be sustainable for fifty years, not five, and the only way to do that was to have it be profitable. While these profits were expected, one of the reasons behind them was not: these outcast students were actually more productive than some of their adult peers at Southwire's other facilities.

Since the inception of 12 for Life, the county's dropout rate has fallen to 22 percent; the program has exceeded the number of projected graduates several times over; and the young men and women are leading independent lives after graduation. The program has sent 40 percent of its students to college or technical school, 30 percent into the military, and 20 percent right into the workforce, many of these at Southwire itself. It's a model that works, and it's been replicated across Georgia and has also been the subject of a Harvard Business School study.

On another trip I visited Worcester Technical High School in Worcester, Massachusetts. Worcester Tech's story was a classic one of school turnaround through sheer force of will on the part of its principal, Sheila Harrity, who would go on to win the 2014 National High School Principal of the Year award. When Ms. Harrity took the reins, Worcester Tech was one of the lowest-performing schools in the state, but she completely revitalized it. She embraced the school's vocational bent, breathing life into the woodworking, automotive, and culinary programs, but she went much further. Ms. Harrity wanted her kids to have different kinds of educational and vocational opportunities; she wanted them to see more of what the world offered after high school. So she partnered with a local credit union and opened a bank branch *inside the school*. A veterinary clinic set up shop, placing a full-time vet right in the building. They launched a philanthropic program helping cancer patients suffering from hair loss to find and receive free wigs. Students could intern in these programs as well as go to traditional classes. By reimagining her school's place in the community and in her students' lives, Ms. Harrity engaged hundreds of teens in ways they hadn't been engaged before. During her tenure, the school went from poor to exceptional, winning a coveted National Blue Ribbon award from the US Department of Education in 2013. Even though it was still a vocational school, as opposed to a high-achieving STEM school or a school concentrating on the humanities, graduation rates soared and so did the proportion of students going to college. Here was a school that had been on the verge of being closed, and one that many in the community had learned to shun. Yet all of that changed under Ms. Harrity. Whether your car needed to be fixed, or your cat was sick, or you needed to cash a check, or you needed a wig because you were going through chemo, you knew exactly where to go: Worcester Tech.

In Baltimore, Maryland, I visited Liberty Elementary in the northwest part of the city. It was akin to any number of Chicago schools on the South and West Sides where poverty, drugs, and violence raged outside on the streets, and it was right in the same neighborhood where Freddie Gray had been arrested and died in police custody. Unlike Worcester Tech, Liberty was a STEM school, and it made a point of putting an iPad in the hands of every student. Middle- and upper-class families might take for granted how special it was for kids to have access to tablets, but we never did, and the principal at Liberty Elementary, Joe Manko, didn't either. Like Ms. Harrity in Worcester, Mr. Manko had transformed his school into a community hub. When the school's rec center was slated for demolition by city budget cuts, he rallied the neighborhood and saved it. But the rec center didn't only host basketball games; it also housed tutoring and GED classes. Joe went further, though, adding something I'd never seen: he turned the rec center into a food bank that handed out 16,000 pounds of free food every week. A lot of it went right into the homes of students' families, alleviating the hunger pangs that had previously twisted plenty of young stomachs at his school. I'm sure this was not in Principal Manko's job description nor in any employee handbook. Mr. Manko and his team simply saw a community need and addressed it. Because of this level of commitment, his school, in one of the toughest and most poverty-ravaged parts of the city, was one of the highest-achieving schools in Baltimore.

I've had the privilege to see more great public schools across America than maybe anyone else. Each one had its own story, but this is what they all had in common: they had great leaders and teachers, they found ways to serve their children and their community, and they made their students feel special and valued. I can't provide data that proves that having a veterinary clinic in a high school leads to higher graduation rates, or that handing out 16,000 pounds of food every week leads to better student achievement, but I *know* that they do.

Meanwhile, as I crisscrossed the nation, visiting all these schools, Race to the Top was under way. Right from the beginning it exceeded our expectations. It was like a wave breaking across the country, capturing the imaginations of nearly every governor and key leaders at the state level. Unions were mostly amenable to reforms, nonprofits lined up to help, private investors and the business community clamored for change, and both red and blue states were primed. The governors principally wanted three things: better educations for their students, making their states more competitive in the long run; a way to address the shortcomings of No Child Left Behind; and more stimulus money as state budgets groaned under the strains of the Great Recession.

I received the first sheet of final scores in late March 2010. All I knew about the states at that point was which ones had chosen *not* to compete. Alaska, North Dakota, Texas, and Vermont opted out, and none of them would compete in any future round. In the first round these were joined by Maine, Maryland, Mississippi, Montana, Nevada, and Washington—all of which would compete in later rounds (and one of which would win $250 million). The remaining forty states from Alabama to Wyoming, plus the District of Columbia, each submitted an application. We'd named sixteen finalists and now had the end results. Based on the scores, there were two clear winners with a natural break between them and the rest of the pack. I just didn't know which states they were.

States	Phase 1	Phase 2	Phase 3
Alabama	Participant	Participant	
Alaska			
Arizona	Participant	Finalist	Awarded $25 million
Arkansas	Participant	Participant	
California	Participant	Finalist	Invited
Colorado	Finalist	Finalist	Awarded $18 million
Connecticut	Participant	Participant	
Delaware	Awarded $100 million		
DC	Finalist	Awarded $75 million	
Florida	Finalist	Awarded $700 million	
Georgia	Finalist	Awarded $400 million	
Hawaii	Participant	Awarded $75 million	
Idaho	Participant		
Illinois	Finalist	Finalist	Awarded $43 million
Indiana	Participant	Participant	
Iowa	Participant	Participant	
Kansas	Participant		
Kentucky	Finalist	Finalist	Awarded $17 million
Louisiana	Finalist	Finalist	Awarded $17 million
Maine		Participant	
Maryland		Awarded $250 million	

States	Phase 1	Phase 2	Phase 3
Massachusetts	Finalist	Awarded $250 million	
Michigan	Participant	Participant	
Minnesota	Participant		
Mississippi		Participant	
Missouri	Participant	Participant	
Montana		Participant	
Nebraska	Participant	Participant	
Nevada		Participant	
New Hampshire	Participant	Participant	
New Jersey	Participant	Finalist	Awarded $38 million
New Mexico	Participant	Participant	
New York	Finalist	Awarded $700 million	
North Carolina	Finalist	Awarded $400 million	
North Dakota			
Ohio	Finalist	Awarded $400 million	
Oklahoma	Participant	Participant	
Oregon	Participant		
Pennsylvania	Finalist	Finalist	Awarded $41 million
Rhode Island	Finalist	Awarded $75 million	
South Carolina	Finalist	Finalist	Invited
South Dakota	Participant		
Tennessee	Awarded $100 million		
Texas			
Utah	Participant	Participant	

States	Phase 1	Phase 2	Phase 3
Vermont			
Virginia	Participant		
Washington		Participant	
West Virginia	Participant		
Wisconsin	Participant	Participant	
Wyoming	Participant		

"All right, who do we have?" I asked.

I rarely get nervous, but I absolutely was in that moment. The Race enjoyed bipartisan support, but I knew Washington politics could turn toxic on a dime. In those early months of 2010, the Tea Party was still nascent, but it was rumbling. In time, it would come full force at the president, the Race, me, and the Department of Education. At the extreme it would even come for the notion of free, public education, although we weren't there yet. Obama was getting pushed hard on his health care initiative, but at the Department we were still very much in the honeymoon period. The success of the Race and how it was perceived would go a long way in determining how long that honeymoon could last.

If our two winners were large blue states, like New York and California, it would be over quickly. We'd be unable to avoid accusations of political gamesmanship, and it wouldn't matter how transparent we'd been: facts would be twisted and political bones would be picked over by packs of staffers sent down from the Hill.

It would probably have been better if our two states were red, like Georgia and Kentucky. But I knew that would create similar problems on our left flank, opening us to accusations that our ideas were nothing more than repackaged right-of-center nonsense.

Two purple states, like Ohio and Florida, might have been ideal, but awarding them might make it look like we were showering resources on a pair of swing states that had, in essence, won the presidency for Obama. No one would be quiet about that outcome.

As I pondered all this, someone said, "The winners are Delaware and Tennessee, Arne."

Delaware and Tennessee—one blue, one red. When I heard them, I was both stunned and immensely relieved. Tennessee had always performed near the bottom of the pack nationally, and Delaware was at best mediocre. I knew instantly that these two states would see an infusion of cash for education like they had never seen before, and that the children of those states would likely see a dramatic improvement in the quality of their educations. (Time has proved that this optimism was not completely misplaced.) I also realized our team had hit the lottery: having those two states win was a perfect way not for our work to end but for it to begin.

I wanted to know more about our winners, so the team briefed me. Delaware was serious about reform. They'd vaulted into first place after their presentation, which was personally led by their governor, Democrat Jack Markell. Joining him was their state education officer, a district superintendent, the president of the Delaware chapter of the National Education Association, and a local businessman who was deep into school reform (and also a staunch Republican, it turned out). The reviewers learned that these five people were a true team who knew what they were talking about. Every district, as well as every local union chapter, had signed a letter supporting the state's reform plans, and we discovered that Governor Markell had even convened meetings *before* the Race was announced to address many of the same education issues we were attempting to tackle.

Tennessee had a long history of reform efforts, especially when it came to using data to assess teachers. Led by Governor Phil Bredesen, a Democrat who was on his way out of the statehouse due to term limits, Tennessee showed that their teacher evaluation reforms would be carried out statewide, not just in select districts. "We said at the outset it's all or nothing," Bredesen said. "We're past the point of demonstration projects or pilot projects." Another thing distinguishing Tennessee—and that I was aware of, since it was public knowledge—was that Governor Bredesen had gotten every single gubernatorial candidate, Republican and Democrat, to sign a pledge binding them to enact any and all Race to the Top reforms as governor. I thought this was a stroke of genius. I'd never heard of any politician getting all of their potential successors across the political spectrum to agree to anything, let alone something as hard as improving public education. His successor, Republican Bill Haslam, would turn out to be phenomenal and hold up every corner of that pledge.

While it was great that our two winners were a blue and a red state, it was even better that they were both relatively small. Tennessee counted 846,000 students, and Delaware, whose physical area is twenty-one times smaller than Tennessee's, had a mere 126,000 students. What this meant was that our two winners wouldn't break the bank. Delaware ended up with about $107 million, while Tennessee got about $500 million. This allowed us to keep most of our ammunition dry, leaving us with more than $3 billion for round two. (We'd also carved out $350 million for a parallel competition for developing better assessments.) The states that hadn't won saw that we were serious, and also that there was a ton of money left on the table, all of which we had promised to give out in round two. These two things combined to unleash a second wave of reform across the nation that was even stronger than the first. (A third and much smaller round was financed by additional money allocated by Congress in the spring of 2011.)

I was also extremely happy because these two states would insulate us from political attack. It felt like validation for a well-designed system, and Joanne and her team deserved all the credit for that. If we'd made our decisions based solely on politics, then why on earth would we pick Delaware or Tennessee? We wouldn't. That was proof enough that the process was fair and apolitical.

Our honeymoon period was extended, and it remained largely intact over the next few months as we took round two applications, right up to June 1. But as the 2010 midterms loomed, and as American politics ramped into its preelection silly season, we began to see some hints of unrest. The first shot across the bow

STRANGE
BEDFELLOWS

Unlike Jack Markell, Chris Christie didn't attend his state's Race presentation. Instead, the lead was his state education officer, Bret Schundler. The deadline for filing the submission for round two was June 1, and New Jersey had had to produce a *second* application because on May 27 Governor Christie took issue with a union-related provision in the first version of the application. This meant that his state's officials had to scramble over the Memorial Day weekend to get the application right. (Memorial Day in New Jersey, with its miles of beaches and proximity to New York, Philly, and DC, is about as high a holiday as any.)

New Jersey made the deadline, although only one person was available in Trenton that weekend to review the hundreds of pages of appendices attached to the application. Later in the summer, New Jersey was announced as one of nineteen finalists, each of which was invited to give presentations in DC. New Jersey's delegation showed up on a hot and sticky August day, and at some point a reviewer asked Schundler and his colleagues to explain an error. We requested that each state compare education spending for 2009 to spending in 2008. We expected the amount to drop in 2009 due to the recession, but wanted to see if the percent the state spent on education went up or down—that is, was the state committed to education regardless of the economic downturn? Instead, the New Jersey application compared 2010 dollars to 2011 projections—an exercise that was completely beside the point. Put on the spot, Schundler couldn't explain why this had happened and basically asked for the chance at a do-over.

The reviewer said that wouldn't be possible. New Jersey hadn't provided the correct numbers so they ended up getting docked five points. When all was said and done, the state came in eleventh, missing the tenth and final award-winning spot by exactly three points. New Jersey was out $400 million, which went to Ohio. The other winners, from first to last, were Massachusetts, New York, Hawaii (which was a shock), Florida, Rhode Island, the District of Columbia, Maryland, Georgia, and North Carolina. A nice geographical and political mix of states, plus DC.

Christie was understandably livid, and he let the public know right away. It's useful to remember some context here. This was the summer of 2010. The Tea Party, emboldened by opposition to the Affordable Care Act and, in my opinion, the fact that our president was a black man, was on the rise. When you turned on the news, you'd see signs like "Obama bin Lyin'" and "Somewhere in Kenya a village has lost its idiot" and "Hang in there, Obama," next to which would be a crude picture of a noose. There were plenty of other, less racist signs about taxation and capitalism and issues like health care, but the salient message (and it's the same one that drove Trump into the White House) was that people didn't like "the way things were going." All over, people were saying, "I'm afraid for my country." Not "our" country, "my" country, and the subtext was nearly always racial. The nation was continuing to fray and divide along partisan lines, and the Tea Party was willing to exploit and misdirect people's real, genuine pain to satisfy its appetite for power. Bottom line: while the midterm elections were still a few months away, that August things looked bleaker. The honeymoon we enjoyed at the Department of Education was not likely to last much longer.

To his credit, Christie didn't engage in this kind of racial animus. But while he wasn't up for reelection in the fall of 2010, he knew there was blood in the water. On August 25 he got behind a podium and let New Jerseyites know how he felt. Schundler had apparently told the governor that they'd tried to give the reviewer the correct information, but that they'd been rebuffed. Christie said, "When the president comes back to New Jersey, he's going to have to explain to the people of the state of New Jersey why he's depriving them of $400 million that this application earned. Because one of his bureaucrats in Washington couldn't pick up the phone and ask a question, couldn't go on the Internet and find information, or wouldn't accept the verbal representation of Commissioner Schundler when they were down there." This wasn't exactly accurate.

This example of bare-knuckle politicking took place on a Wednesday. On Thursday we released the video of New Jersey's presentation. (Whoever it was on our Race to the Top team that insisted on taping every meeting was a genius.) It directly contradicted Governor Christie's assertion that we'd denied them a chance to fix the error. It showed that Schundler and his team were both unaware of the error and that they were so ignorant of their own application that they couldn't address it in real time. Schundler was fired the next day, and Christie felt compelled to make another statement. He didn't exactly apologize to the president, but he did express regret that he'd been given bad (that is, false) information from his officials. For our part, I hoped we had demonstrated to the other states and governors that the Race was absolutely operating in good faith.

(Things got weirder and more fascinating that weekend in the Garden State. First, Schundler insisted that he hadn't lied to the governor and that he'd told him exactly what had happened, implying it was the governor who was obfuscating all along. Then, the *Star-Ledger*, a Newark-based paper, reported that the original application, which Christie had nullified, had the *correct* information for 2008 and 2009; only because of the hasty rewrite he demanded had the numbers changed. Lost in the fog was that New Jersey had lost a lot more than five points for its inability to convince many of the local teachers' unions to agree to reform, and this was probably the real culprit for their losing out. The unions, perhaps disingenuously, blamed Christie, and Christie blamed his officials as well as the unions. No one in a position of influence seemed to step up and say *My bad.* Perhaps the strangest development involved the dismissal of Schundler, who refused to resign and requested he be terminated so he could collect unemployment benefits. This from a leading New Jersey Republican who in the past had advocated for welfare reform!)

New Jersey's peculiar problems notwithstanding, I was amazed that so many states had taken Race to the Top seriously and that most of the country had coalesced around the majority of its ideas. It was far better than we'd expected and it felt great, but with round two complete we were now out of funds. We would eventually get a little more for a third round, but from that moment on we shifted from encouraging reform to doing whatever we could to help the states carry it out.

Unfortunately, our problems were just beginning. To be clear, some of our biggest ones were absolutely self-inflicted, and I'm happy to take the blame for them. But the multiple inaccuracies that Christie was willing to tell that ended up disparaging the Department of Education, and by extension the president, should have served notice that we be on the lookout for more and bigger lies, which would come at us sooner than later.

Not long after the New Year, I got a call from another Republican governor on my personal cell phone. It was a Saturday morning and it came as I walked home from the store in our neighborhood, carrying some eggs and a carton of milk.

"Hello?" I said.

"Hi—is this Secretary Duncan?" a man asked. His voice had that clear, no-nonsense quality that many busy people possess.

"It is. Who's this?"

"Secretary Duncan, this is Governor Kasich. From Ohio."

I knew who John Kasich was but I'd never spoken to him or anyone on his staff, so I was a little surprised. "Oh, hey, Governor. Congratulations on your election win."

"Thank you, Mr. Secretary—"

"Please, Governor, it's Arne."

"All right—Arne. And thank you, about the win."

"My pleasure. What can I do for you, Governor Kasich?"

"Listen, this is about Ohio's Race to the Top award."

"Congratulations on that too, by the way."

"I hope so. I don't know how much you know about me, but I served in Congress and I know how these things work."

"All right," I said, not sure where this was going.

"Are we still going to get our money?" he asked, cutting right to it.

"Excuse me?"

"Ohio's outgoing governor was a Democrat and I'm a Republican, so are we still going to get our money? I know all this stuff is about politics, Arne. I don't live under a rock."

I took a moment before answering. "Governor Kasich, I'm sorry, but this is a hard way to start a relationship."

"A relationship?" he asked in disbelief.

"Yes. With due respect, you don't know me either, not from a bar of soap. Of course you're going to get your money, so long as you stick to your state's plan. You guys already won. Even if I or the president wanted to hold back funds to grind some kind of ax, which we don't, we couldn't do it. You may think this is about politics, but it isn't."

"So we'll still get funded?"

"Yes. You have my word. You should already have the first chunk."

"Yeah, we do. I just want to make sure you won't renege."

I chose to ignore that. "If you don't mind my asking, has anyone briefed you on how the Race was set up?"

"Yes."

I stopped walking and gave him my full attention. "If you'll let me, I'd like to go through it again with you. Ask around—the governors are my guys. I'm here for you, to help your kids. I want you to trust us, and believe me when I say that I have zero interest in politics." That seemed to get his attention. He listened as I outlined the workings of the Race: the peer reviews, the score averaging, and how we picked winners blind. I assured him we were not picking favorites or handing out gifts. I also assured him that we weren't mandating anything—that we were just providing incentives that we hoped would create a sea change in how American public education worked. "Because right now, it isn't working all that well," I added.

When I was finished he said, "It sounds like you know what

you're talking about, I'll give you that." I wouldn't say he sounded convinced about everything, but he did seem to be less skeptical.

Before we hung up I said, "We'll be doing other competitions in the future, Governor. We have an early-learning competition going, and we have some other, smaller competitions in the works. Point being, there's more money out there to help you guys do what you think is right for kids. I want to work with everyone. I don't care if your entire state is registered Republican, I'm here to help you. You have my number. Please use it."

That was the beginning of what would eventually grow into a friendship based upon mutual respect. Governor Kasich has turned out to be a prime example of a profile in political courage when it comes to education reform, standing up for and defending the Common Core State Standards against many of his Republican peers and constituents. I don't agree with Governor Kasich on every matter of policy, but I know his heart is in the right place and that he will fight for the educations of Ohio's children.

Over the next few years I doubled down with the governors, staying in contact with each of them, even the ones who didn't like me all that much. For the most part these relationships were productive, but as Christie and Kasich showed, the winds were shifting across the country—winds that gathered and ultimately blew in on a tempest for the 2016 presidential election. The "shellacking," as Obama called it, that Democrats took in the 2010 midterms made the work feel that much *more* urgent, so we kept moving. There was a ton of stuff for the states to put in place: higher standards, assessments to match these, new curriculum, data systems, and accountability structures, to name but a few. A lot of ink has justifiably been spilled on these subjects, but I want to zero in on one that got a lot of attention: standards. The Race supported and accelerated an existing movement to raise state academic standards. Most states still use these standards today, or a version that's been rebranded as a statewide product, like the Florida Sunshine State Standards or the Tennessee Academic Standards.

Before all that happened, though, they were simply referred to as the Common Core.

The Common Core State Standards are close to universally known, and almost as misunderstood. A little history is in order, then.

In December 2008, before Obama's inauguration, the National Governors Association and the Council of Chief State School Officers, along with a nonprofit called Achieve, Inc., issued a report titled *Benchmarking for Success: Ensuring U.S. Students Receive a World-Class Education*. In this they held that states should "upgrade state standards by adopting a common core of internationally benchmarked standards in math and language arts for grades K–12." I'm pretty sure this is the source of the name "Common Core." (Interestingly, nowhere in any of the original Common Core material is the word "federal" found—except in reference to the *Federalist Papers* as an example of what a high schooler might read in English class—and nowhere in any of the Race to the Top rules will you find the phrase "Common Core.")

The genesis of the Common Core went even further back, to

a bipartisan group of governors in the 1990s who came together and, among other things, called for higher standards nationwide. From that moment, governors, college professors, education officers, and teachers—not to mention students and their parents—were becoming increasingly aware of a huge problem: high school graduates were getting into college only to find that they were not remotely prepared for college-level work. This had been a trend before No Child Left Behind, and after that law's passage it continued as some states lowered their definitions of "proficiency" so that more kids would pass the tests, allowing those states to appear to be meeting benchmarks. Earlier I talked about this exact phenomenon in Illinois, but it was by no means confined to my home state.

Since community colleges and four-year universities were not in the business of dumbing down coursework, an increasing number of kids were showing up as freshmen who needed to retake high school classes. (To take but one example, in 2011 more than *68 percent* of Tennessee's incoming community college freshmen needed at least one remedial class!) Many of these students were using financial aid dollars to pay for these classes, which earn students no college credit, and many of these students ended up dropping out. College debt is a massive problem in this country, but the truth is that the vast majority of college graduates will be able to pay back their student loans. The truly insidious trap is for those who incur debt but earn no degree. They are much more likely to default, causing disruptive ripples throughout their lives.

Before Obama took office, the states had concluded that the

standards *had* to change for the better. They didn't need to be lowered to make governors look good under No Child Left Behind; they needed to be higher so that more students knew more things, No Child Left Behind be damned. It wasn't that the governors wanted to improve standards in order to engage in some sort of experiment—it was that the need for change was painfully evident. In the words of Governor Markell, "The bargain had been broken." Once again we were lying to our kids about the state of their educations.

The creation of the Common Core State Standards had taken place over the course of a few years, and the states were lucky to have them available when we began Race to the Top. The people who created the standards used the rallying cry of "Fewer, clearer, higher." (In the words of David Coleman, one of the lead authors of the Common Core, the previous standards had been created with too many cooks in the kitchen and were "a mile wide and an inch deep.") The goal of the new standards was to determine what needed to be known at each grade level.

In math, this boiled down to numeracy, arithmetic, and basic mathematical understanding. "There is a world of difference between a student who can summon a mnemonic device to expand a product such as $(a + b)(x + y)$ and a student who can explain where the mnemonic comes from," reads part of the introduction to the Common Core math standards.

In English Language Arts, this boiled down to being able to read and understand *any* text written in English, and then write about that text using evidence. "The Standards . . . lay out a vision of what it means to be a literate person in the twenty-first century," reads the corresponding introduction to the English standards. These standards also tried to "demonstrate the . . . use of evidence that is essential to both private deliberation and responsible citizenship in a democratic republic." Mirroring our democracy, a lot of people from all backgrounds came together in good faith to produce these standards. Unfortunately, also mirroring our democracy, some of the politics that sprouted up around the Common Core were poisonous and divisive.

Because Race to the Top was a federal program that encouraged shared higher standards among the states, and because the Common Core State Standards were available as the Race was happening, critics of the Common Core conflated them with federal overreach. After the battle for health care reform, or Obamacare, the standards got tagged "Obamacore." This was not a favorable nickname. For critics who latched onto it, "Obamacore" amounted to a federal takeover of educational standards and curriculum, even though neither was true. (Regarding curriculum, the standards said as much: "These Standards do not dictate curriculum or teaching methods." That fact didn't seem to matter.)

A simple Google search turns up a lot of critical stuff from the right about the Common Core. Phyllis Schlafly, the well-known conservative commentator, said, "Obama Core [sic] is a comprehensive plan to dumb down schoolchildren so they will be obedient servants of the government and probably to indoctrinate them to accept the leftwing view of America and its history." Glenn

Beck said, "This is the progressive movement coming in for the kill. And believe me, if we don't stop it, this will be the kill." Rush Limbaugh, in his magazine's Nailing the Left column, called the Common Core "Stupid. Confusing. Destructive." I bet none of these commentators took the time to read the standards, but that didn't prevent them from chiming in.

As time went on I tried to brush off these kinds of statements and stay above the political fray. I kept coming back to what President Obama said to me: "Just do what you think is right for kids and let me worry about the politics." I was content to do just that. But every now and then the politics were unavoidable.

One exchange I'll never forget happened over dinner at a fancy DC restaurant with the Republican senator Lamar Alexander from Tennessee. Senator Alexander was a former secretary of education under George H. W. Bush, and had been the governor of Tennessee. He and I had a good and cordial working relationship, and at my confirmation hearing he'd been one of my most generous supporters, saying, "I am very impressed by what you have been able to accomplish and what you have been able to do." In his view, I was one of several "distinguished" cabinet appointments that President Obama had made. I appreciated that and was proud to hear it.

Senator Alexander was also proud of Tennessee, which was already using its Race award to make progress. At some point the conversation turned to tying teacher evaluation to student test scores, an initiative generally opposed by Democrats and the teachers' unions but one that Senator Alexander had long been pursuing.

"That is the Holy Grail of ed reform, Arne," I recall him saying.

"I agree that it's important, Senator," I said. "But it'd be meaningless without higher standards too. All of it's important."

"True, but that one is tough. Really tough. I tried to do it twenty years ago, but couldn't."

"Well, I think that Governor Haslam is doing great."

"Yes. Yes, he is. . . . But, Arne, I'm sorry. I can't support you and the president on it."

He looked me right in the eye as he said this, and I knew he meant it. I appreciated his honesty, but I was stunned. Senator Alexander knew the challenges of education policy better than most people on the Hill. He knew that no governor nor any previous administration had accomplished what we were about to accomplish. He knew how important the issue of accountability was—in his own words it was the "Holy Grail of ed reform." Despite that, he was content to label it "federal overreach" and not support our efforts to break through. I felt this was the Tea Party talking, pure and simple. It was as if he'd been captured. The president was up for reelection that year, and the Republican Party wanted him defeated more than anything. This meant opposing him at every turn. Senator Alexander's stance on this issue exemplified what was so often broken in DC politics: here ideology and the quest for power were trumping what he knew was in the best interest of children. Incidentally, his stance also ran precisely counter to what his own Republican governor wanted and was in the process of doing anyway.

Was teacher evaluation and testing controversial? Of course. But these things were mostly opposed by people on the left, not the right. Their critiques weren't as crazy-sounding as those of Limbaugh or Beck, but they were just as passionate. In general, Democrats and the teachers' unions supported the Common Core, as well as the curriculum that the states were developing to teach to these higher standards—but they were opposed to doing anything that tied teacher evaluation to student learning. This was a bridge too far; it was exactly what Obama got booed for back in 2008. For the unions, as well as for many Democrats, teacher accountability was the third rail.

We absolutely made some mistakes here. Our Department of Education could have done more to help the states communicate *why* annual testing was important for students and teachers. We could have talked a lot more about why, collectively, we needed to build confidence in public education; and the only way to do that was by being willing to hold ourselves accountable. We also might have encouraged the states to roll out reforms differently. Some on our team advocated for a more incremental approach. They argued that first the states could adopt higher standards and wait a few years while the curriculum caught up and teachers developed new skills; then the states could start testing students, but not let those scores count for anything for a few more years while the kinks got ironed out; then, a few years later, they could finally fold in the teacher evaluation component. While the people who favored this approach knew it could take ten or more years and span multiple administrations, they believed this was the best way.

I heard them and understood their viewpoint, but I simply didn't agree. Each difficult change inevitably would have been punted further down the road, and in the end, nothing would improve. Students would still be shortchanged, the country would continue to fall behind its international peers, and there would still be plenty of political pushback. For me, then, it was all or nothing. (Actually, if I had to do it all over again, I would push even harder than we did; there's never a "right" time for fundamental change.)

The story revolving around teacher evaluation and testing got complicated and ugly pretty quickly, especially once actual test results started coming in. The general problem: they were low, in some cases really low. Since the standards were higher and the tests different, this was to be expected, but it was still a shock, especially around desks and at dinner tables. All of a sudden, students thought they weren't doing so well, parents were worried their kids' schools weren't good enough, and teachers were getting judged on the results. Some of those teachers panicked. Some asked, "How can we stop this?"

One way to stop it was to become strange bedfellows with those on the right, who hated anything Obama touched. Our critics on the left promptly rallied around their opposition to the tests that resulted from the Common Core (even though they were in favor of these higher standards), and, like the right, tried to conflate and confuse things to reach narrow political ends.

All of this came to a head when I infamously jammed my foot in my mouth one Friday in November 2013. I was at a meeting with state school superintendents, where I said, "It's fascinating to me that some of the pushback is coming from, sort of, white suburban moms who—all of a sudden—their child isn't as brilliant as they thought they were and their school isn't quite as good as they thought they were, and that's pretty scary. You've bet your house and where you live and everything on 'My child's going to be prepared.' That can be a punch in the gut."

I was talking about a group of parents, initially concentrated in suburban Long Island, New York, but which had spread to other similar places nationwide, who were reacting against the statewide tests their kids were taking. In the previous spring, New York had seen test scores drop by 30 percent. The curriculum was changing, and classwork and homework looked radically different. These changes made people suddenly uncomfortable with their coveted, high-home-value public schools, and some families were choosing to "opt out" of the tests altogether in protest. In some places groupthink settled in and opting out became fashionable. Joanne even told me a story about a friend who called her and asked if her kid should opt out. "Are you kidding?" she replied. "No."

Over that weekend I got pilloried—and for my lack of tact I absolutely deserved it. I was labeled a bigot (against white folks this time); got accused of divisiveness (inserting race and class into any context tends to do that); and of being an aloof and uncaring bureaucrat. I got a pair of well-publicized open letters, one from a school principal, the other from a busy, committed, and very loving mother, both of which argued against the Common Core standards and the tests they had birthed.

This was where we really failed. These folks should have been our natural allies. But because we were miserable at communicating how and why these things were happening, and why they were important, it made things worse. For whatever it's worth, I'm sorry that we contributed to that.

What I would have liked to explain was that all of it was necessary, all at once. The world was changing so quickly, and education wasn't. Think about it: the modern Internet is only about twenty-five years old, we've only been able to use Google search since late 1997, and smartphones have only been around for *ten years*. Can you imagine a world without these things? We were falling behind other countries *before* these innovations transformed our society, but now we were getting absolutely dusted. Our inability to move and innovate in education had cost us dearly, and if we didn't change soon, those losses would compound.

What I would have liked to explain was that opting out doesn't help anyone; it hurts everyone. Yes, the tests are given to individual kids, and families get these results to know how their children are doing. But the results give a picture of the entire system. If a significant chunk of better-off kids opts out, then how can we know how poorer kids are doing? Our skewed and broken system rewards wealthier kids, schools, and districts, while it simultaneously harms poorer ones. It's *designed* this way, and that's partly what we were attempting to fix.

What I also would've liked to have explained more clearly was that while annual assessments were important, many districts and states were over-testing their students. In education, we're great at starting new things, but not very good at stopping old ones. Eventually, the Department encouraged states to reduce the amount of testing, but we were late getting there.

Lastly, I would have liked to explain—or, rather, stressed—that, at the end of the day, education is a human endeavor. We can talk about all these things—standards, assessments, curriculum, data, etc.—until we're blue in the face, but if we don't have great teachers, then none of it matters. I would have explained that one path to more great teachers all across the country is to have the ability to evaluate them, to know who's doing a great job, who's still developing and needs more support, and who's not doing well at all. I would also have explained that tests, while imperfect, are one essential component of that evaluation.

I lost some sleep during my years in DC: it's a tough town, and we definitely made mistakes while I was there. But, at least when it comes to things like Race to the Top, I don't lose sleep anymore. It's not inaccurate to say that Race to the Top changed the education landscape in America. According to Governor Haslam, with whom I recently spoke, President Obama's greatest lasting achievement was the work his administration spearheaded in education. I hope he's right. In any case, since Race to the Top, forty-six states, Washington DC, and the Department of Defense Education Activity, which oversees all K–12 schools on military bases around the world, have either adopted Common Core outright or developed their own high standards. Because the states developed these and put them in place—and not the federal government, as some erroneously believe—they will not easily be taken away or dumbed down by current or future administrations. My hope is that in the future our country will be better for them.

The end of the introduction to the Common Core State Standards for English Language Arts & Literacy puts it pretty well, I think. It reads, "These Standards are not intended to be new names for old ways of doing business. They are a call to take the next step. It is time for states to work together to build on lessons learned from two decades of standards based reforms. It is time to recognize that standards are not just promises to our children, but promises we intend to keep."

TWENTY-FIVE POUNDS OF APPLES AND THREE POUNDS OF CHEESE

When I was in my late twenties and early thirties, long after I'd given up playing pro basketball, I got an opportunity to learn things about the game I'd never understood before. My teachers included my old friends John Rogers Jr. and Craig Robinson. Both had played for the Princeton Tigers under Hall of Fame coach Pete Carril, and Craig has made his career coaching and working in professional basketball.

When I returned from Australia in 1992, the three of us started playing around the county in the three-on-three Hoop It Up tournament, recruiting a couple of other Princeton standouts who were a little younger than us. Their names were Sean Jackson and Kit Mueller. Sean was the Ivy League Player of the Year in

1992, and Kit, who was Princeton's all-time second leading scorer behind NBA Hall of Famer and former senator Bill Bradley, had played pro ball overseas for a while. We also had a few other guys on our squad from Northwestern. We worked hard to learn how to play together, and over the years we've been fortunate enough to win several championships. I continued to play in these games as well as in a couple celebrity games at the NBA All-Star Weekend throughout my time at the Department of Education.

What I learned from these guys was a system called the Princeton Offense. Basketball is often associated with the exploits of a single player—Michael Jordan, LeBron James, Steph Curry—but the nuances of the game lie in teamwork and constant movement. The ball can move faster than any player, whether it's slung overhand down the length of the court or needled through the legs and arms of defenders with a spot-on bounce pass. This law of basketball physics can be exploited by a group of five players who each possess above-average (but not necessarily great) skill at passing, dribbling, and shooting. In this system, there aren't set positions like guard and forward, and there's no true point guard to run the offense. The *entire unit* is the offense.

In the Princeton Offense players constantly cut and move and set picks (this is when a player uses his body to stop or "pick" an opposing player from moving in a certain direction in order to free up a teammate). The guys work through plays they've drilled thousands of times with the goal of getting the best possible shot. If it's a layup off a back-door cut—the system's signature play—then it's often uncontested and an easy score. If it's a three-pointer off a pass out of a double team, then the shot is riskier but the reward is greater. More than likely this three is a wide-open look, and since everyone on the floor can shoot, it's worth attempting.

If you're a basketball fan, this will all sound pretty familiar. Big data has infiltrated the world of sports, and advanced analytics have proved what Carril knew intuitively back in the 1970s and 1980s: that a layup or dunk is the best shot in basketball, that an open three-pointer is the second-best shot, and that mid-range two-pointers are far and away the worst. If possible, it's better to take a pair of free throws than to snap off a feathery eighteen-footer. This is the game as it's played today, but this is how Princeton has played for decades.

And they've been very successful. Under Carril, the Tigers won thirteen Ivy League Championships and were invited to the NCAA tournament eleven times, far more than any other Ivy League school. Because the offense has a slower pace, and because their players are committed defenders, the Tigers also led the nation nineteen times in scoring defense (the ability to hold opposing teams to the lowest number of points). So long as everyone's willing to pass, it's a brilliant system, and to my mind the best way to play the game.

What I've learned is that basketball is a classroom, and that's where I found myself when I started to play with John, Craig, Kit, and Sean. I was lucky enough to play in college and professionally overseas, but I quickly discovered that I had a ton of bad habits. I was used to playing with guys who took turns with the ball, or at most who took turns playing basic two-man games with a guard and big man. Dump it into the paint and then sprint, or "cut," toward the basket and hope for a pass and a decent shot closer to the rim. Or set a good pick, hope the defender goes underneath it, and take a quick, open shot. The way I'd played meant that guys' roles were more defined: this guy boxed out for a rebound; this guy slashed to the basket; this guy took mid-range shots; this guy dunked; this guy camped out in the corner, waiting for the ball to swing to him so he could launch a three.

When I started learning from my friends, I realized that the difference between what I knew about basketball and what they knew was stark. They taught me how to space the floor. They taught me to cut *away* from the ball, not toward it. They taught me when to leave a pick: if it was too soon or too late, I'd miss the chance for an open shot. They taught me that "waiting" for the ball meant moving, not standing still while another player dribbled around defenders. On defense, they taught me how to coax opposing players into positions they didn't like; how to push them out of their comfort zone; and how to force them to take bad shots that they didn't even know were bad. There's a huge difference percentage-wise between a two-foot layup and an eight-foot layup, and we always tried to get them to take that eight-footer.

Most of this instruction ran counter to everything I'd internalized about the game. It was hard to unlearn and relearn things. We did thousands of drills. Start, stop, start, stop. We slowed the game down and literally walked through plays in order to get the timing right. It was hugely frustrating, and more than anything I remember failing over and over and over again. It was also strange to learn that I'd been doing things wrong for so many years.

Pushing oneself to do things differently in any endeavor is hard work, and the goal with all this instruction and repetition was to stop the mind from interfering. I had to dig out my bad habits and replace them with good ones. If thought came into the picture—if I said to myself, *Okay, I'll cut to the basket in one more second*—then I was cooked. But if we practiced the plays enough, and if we internalized the concepts behind them, then our minds no longer had to tell our bodies what to do and when. It was at that moment that things would click.

Eventually they did. I'll never forget when I first beat a teammate back door off a perfect bounce pass. The guy guarding me was caught flat-footed, and when I hit my spot the ball was right there in my hands. I can still see the backboard and the leading edge of the rim as the ball rolled from my fingertips, caromed off the glass, and slipped through the net.

I'm telling this story about practice, repetition, trust, frustration, failure, and ultimately success, because this is what great teaching and learning looks like. I'd seen master teachers practice their craft in so many different settings: classrooms, science labs, debate classes, and basketball courts, to name a few. However, one critique of me was that I had never been a classroom teacher. But the truth was I thought of myself as a teacher, albeit one who'd learned the craft in unusual ways, starting as a ten-year-old in my mom's program who was given a group of six- and seven-year-olds to teach how to add and subtract.

This observation that I was not a certified educator went hand in glove with the idea that the changes the Department favored were somehow anti-teacher. Trying to convince teachers that I understood the challenges of their job, and that I was wildly *pro*-teacher, was a constant struggle.

It came to a public head in May 2011, when, during Teacher Appreciation Week, I posted an open letter to America's teachers on the Department's website. In it I praised teachers for taking a difficult and often thankless job that could also be one of the most fulfilling professions on the planet. I wrote to them that "you are frustrated when teachers alone are blamed for educational failures that have roots in broken families, unsafe communities, misguided reforms, and underfunded school systems. You rightfully believe that responsibility for educational quality should be shared by administrators, community, parents, and even students themselves." I ended the letter by saying simply, "I hear you, I value you, and I respect you."

The letter did not go over very well.

Many teachers responded critically, online and elsewhere, and very few of them missed the opportunity to point out that I'd never held court in front of a class of unruly seventh graders. True, but they didn't know that my sister and I had started guiding, mentoring, and teaching our Dreamers when they were in seventh grade, and that we stayed with them for six years. With her and John Rogers Jr. I'd also helped open the Ariel Community Academy, a Chicago public school, in 1996. When I was at CPS, I spearheaded a teacher's residency program and had been intimately involved in starting the Academy for Urban School Leadership, an accredited teacher training program, in 2001. When I was in DC, we continued a teacher ambassadors program started under Secretary Spellings that brought in educators from around the country to help us shape policy. But maybe more important than any of these things, I'd seen what my mother, Sue Duncan, had been able to do. What I witnessed every day growing up was how much great teaching matters.

One of the lies here is one that any reasonable person under duress might tell themselves, and it's that they can't make a difference. More than anything, teachers need resources, yet in America they are consistently starved of them. (Look no further than the 2018 teacher strikes taking place across the country, especially in Republican-controlled states, where teachers are rightfully demanding more money and respect.) Teachers in poorer schools regularly use their own money to pay for supplies. Classrooms in affluent neighborhoods are routinely "adopted" by parents to pay for things from pencils to hand wipes. This is shameful, but it's the way our system attempts to function. Without adequate resources and facing all kinds of challenges, some teachers can take a defeatist attitude and check out. The vast majority of teachers are heroes who are defying the odds, but some feel put-upon and can reasonably say *This isn't my fault. I can't fix this, but this is my job, so I'll keep showing up.*

The truth is that they *can* make a difference. I know they can.

The simple fact is that quality teaching matters more than anything. After parents, teachers are the most important people in a child's life. Teachers deserve so much more than they get by way of training, respect, support, and compensation. But I believe that a teacher, like any professional, should also be able and willing—even eager—to demonstrate that she or he is actually *good* at teaching. Furthermore, many great teachers, like many great doctors, thrive in the toughest of situations. It's where they want to be. It's where they're *called* to be. These teachers deserve even more money and respect because of the difference they're making in kids' lives.

Sue Duncan would have had it no other way. She was constantly accountable to her kids, just as they were accountable to her. Her center started in 1961 after she volunteered to teach a Bible study class at Kenwood-Ellis Church. She gathered the kids around at her first class, a little nervous. She was a young white teacher and these were all nine-year-old black girls from the neighborhood. Each child took up a Bible, and Sue instructed them to open it to a certain book and page. She read the first couple verses and then went around the room. What she found was that none of these children could read. They were all in fourth grade, and they were all functionally illiterate.

From there, she decided that it wasn't Bible instruction that was needed but instruction, period. She began an after-school program with virtually no money, getting the church to donate space. She scoured libraries, flea markets, and bookstores for old books. Long before phrases like "cultural competence" were invented, she concentrated on stories that featured African Americans. She made vocabulary flash cards out of cardboard inserts from the dry cleaner. The neighborhood wasn't safe, so she drove some of the kids to the center in our blue station wagon, jamming up to seventeen kids into it and driving so slowly that it used to make me crazy. She eventually took in around eighty kids, from not-yet-year-old babies to young adults in their early twenties. Most kids were in grade school, and the center was always packed to capacity.

She broke the kids into groups and had the older kids tutor the younger ones. A group might include a fifteen-year-old teaching a ten-year-old fractions while the ten-year-old taught a six-year-old how to spell some basic words. She didn't do this purely for lack of resources; she did it because it reflected her philosophy that every kid should be teaching and learning at the same time. Especially for kids coming from tough environments, there was extraordinary power in a ten-year-old knowing that he had the capacity to teach others. For her, learners *were* teachers. She believed that one of a teacher's main academic goals should be to show, through her own example, that teachers never stop learning. I know this is as true today as it was back in 1961.

Sue's writing assignments revolved around personal stories, and Sue got to know many of these kids as if they were her own. The overwhelming majority came from single-parent homes, and virtually all lived below the poverty line. Their world was small and socially isolated. They were confined to North Kenwood/Oakland, often to a few square blocks, and had minimal access to greater Chicago. These kids lived minutes from a world-class science museum but had never been there. They lived a short train ride from downtown Chicago but didn't know that part of the city at all. The eastern border of North Kenwood/Oakland was Lake Michigan, but few had been to the beach. The immediate neighborhood where they spent all of their time was bombed-out and depressed, with vacant, weed-filled lots and hardly any businesses, not counting the drug trade and liquor and corner stores. Because we taught their younger siblings, gang members eventually protected us and our family, but the drug business and the violence it created were omnipresent. People were shot and killed on a regular basis. At home many parents were absent. Some suffered from addiction, and many dads were incarcerated. Nearly everyone—man, woman, and child—carried some measure of personal trauma. This was the reality many of Sue's kids wrote about.

In spite of—or perhaps because of—these circumstances, Sue's main currency was not toughness but love. An old student of hers, Charles Edwards, once told me, "Kids like to know that people really care about them. That's the most important thing, Arne. That's what makes you feel good, only it doesn't happen much at school for kids in Kenwood." Sue tried to remedy that. She was tough, and demanded that everyone follow the rules, but she handed out many more hugs than admonitions. The kids loved her, and she loved them back. Or, as another former student of hers, Ronald Raglin, said, "The most important thing Sue gave us was self-esteem."

She also gave them food. Early on, Sue realized that a lot of the kids in the neighborhood were extremely hungry when they got to the center after school let out. She initially gave them cookies for completing work, but this didn't feel quite right. Hunger shouldn't be something they had to work away, and cookies weren't very healthy. She began coming to the church every day with twenty-five pounds of apples and three pounds of cheese that she got at the Hyde Park food co-op. The kids were able to eat as much as they wanted so long as everyone got a chance to have something. When they left at night, each kid got an orange to take home or eat on the way.

My brother, Owen, and sister, Sarah, and I grew up at Sue's; we were the only white children in the center. I can't tell you how many bags of apples and oranges we carried over the years. But just because we were Sue's children didn't mean we were treated any differently. Unlike our friends at Sue's, our basic needs were being met. We weren't hungry, we had a stable home, and we went to a great school with teachers who cared about us. But at the center we were part of a different and much larger family that loved teaching and learning together, and playing in the gym when we were all done. (Once our lessons were finished and our homework was checked, we were allowed to play kick-baseball and basketball in the church's gym.) For all of us, the center was literally *the center of our lives*.

Growing up, I had two truly great teachers who left lasting impressions on me. One was my high school English teacher, Mrs. McCampbell, who shared two main traits with my mom: she cared a lot and she expected a lot. She helped me learn how to think and how to express myself, and encouraged me to believe that there were no bad ideas. This was before computers, and our papers were usually handwritten in blue ink. The ones I handed in to Mrs. McCampbell always came back covered in red ink, not because I'd done something wrong, but because she'd spent a lot of time crafting thoughtful comments. To get that level of attention—and all of her students got that level of attention—was transformative.

The other great teacher I had during childhood was actually a teenager I met at my mom's center. His name was Kerrie Holley.

Kerrie was about ten years older than me and had been at Sue's since the age of eight. He would stay there for nearly twenty years, first as a student and then as a worker. Through it all, he was a teacher.

Kerrie was a typical kid from the neighborhood, but some of the details of his childhood were extreme even by the standards of the South Side.

He was born at home, the unwanted child of a young mother and a father he'd never meet. The first time he saw his mom was when he went to see her in Dwight Correctional Center, halfway between Chicago and Bloomington, Indiana. For most of Kerrie's childhood his mom was in and out of jail for petty crimes like check fraud and shoplifting. Through it all she was addicted to heroin.

From the first hour of life, Kerrie was raised by his maternal grandmother, a hard-nosed woman from Jim Crow Georgia who was innately distrustful of white people, Sue Duncan included. Kerrie's grandmother's MO in raising children was to do whatever it took to toughen them up, because the world was difficult for everyone but it was especially difficult for little black boys and girls. When she was upset with Kerrie, his grandma reminded him of how she had saved him. After birthing Kerrie in the bathroom, his mother had wrapped him in newspaper and thrown him in the garbage, but his grandma picked him up, peeled off the newspaper, and massaged his premature skin with Vaseline to protect it. Whenever his grandmother was stern he never forgot this tenderness. She protected him, and he lived the first six years of his life invisible to the system, until his grandmother took him to City Hall to get a delayed record of birth.

I'll never forget a story Kerrie once told me about him and his grandma: "I lived on the third floor of a brick house, and riding down the banisters was a fun activity that I did often. On one ride, the stairwell was empty and I slipped and fell three stories. I hit the rails of every floor on my way down and was knocked out cold. When I woke up, my grandmother and several moms stood over me. One of them said, 'We found him like this. He must have fallen.' I opened my eyes and saw my grandmother staring at me in disbelief. She yelled, 'Boy, get up! You ain't hurt!' I moaned and held my head as I struggled to get my feet under me. I can still feel the small knot on the back of my head from the fall. But Grandma didn't care. 'Get up!' she repeated emphatically. 'Stop drawing attention to yourself.' That was how she wanted us to be. Based on her life experience, the only way we'd make it in the world was to be tough and go unnoticed."

Kerrie felt differently, even as a boy. He made himself *very* noticed. Starting at the age of eight, he snuck into the center every day, begging Sue to be officially accepted. She was at capacity, so she refused his pleas. But he was persistent. Eventually my mom relented. Kerrie's grandmother was dubious of letting her grandson go to a white woman's after-school program, but Kerrie had been persistent with her as well. She let him go. If nothing else, she knew he'd be somewhere safe.

Almost immediately upon entering the program, Sue realized that Kerrie was something of a polymath. He was exceptional with numbers and figures, and even though he was always the quietest kid in the room, something about the way he carried himself made him a natural leader. He had no problem sitting at a table with a group of kids, some older than he, and giving them math drills that he cooked up. Kerrie helped me learn how to read and count, and when I was really small I remember sitting in his lap while he read to me as if he were my big brother. For us kids, he became a focus of attention, like a Pied Piper who led us through lessons and into the gym. Kerrie taught me for years. I went on to have great teachers in high school and at Harvard, but I spent more time with Kerrie than with any of them, and none of my other teachers shaped me as profoundly as Kerrie did.

By the age of twelve, Kerrie was Sue's bookkeeper. He balanced the center's checkbook, tracked donations, and helped her manage money. My mom saw so much promise in him that she refused to let him go to the local high school, Martin Luther King, which was large, loud, and violent. She worried it would chew up Kerrie and spit him out, and she didn't want to let that happen.

She also knew Kerrie's older sister had been attacked in a vicious gang fight, and she was worried for his safety. Our neighborhood high school, Kenwood, was less than two miles away but a world apart. So to help, she claimed that Kerrie lived with us, allowing him to attend Kenwood. My mom had many flaws, but she was one of the most ethical people I knew, and it was a little shocking for her to do something like this. It was the only time I can recall my mom lying, but she did it proudly and unequivocally. We received Kerrie's mail for years afterward.

Kerrie excelled at Kenwood, even taking computer programming classes, which was unheard-of in the 1960s. He and another student got so good that they surpassed the teacher and became the student teachers at Kenwood for the computer class.

After graduating from high school, Kerrie went straight into college at DePaul in downtown Chicago. He got his first degree in mathematics and computer science, and his second in law. All the while, up to the age of twenty-eight, he worked with my mom as her right hand. Not until he'd been offered a job at IBM in California did he finally leave. He went on to have an illustrious career, securing multiple patents, publishing books, spearheading an analytics and machine learning portfolio at Cisco, and now leads an artificial intelligence team at Optum as United Health Group's first Technology Fellow. At IBM, he became the first African American to earn the Distinguished Engineer award, and only the second African American to be named a Fellow in IBM's one-hundred-year history. Pretty remarkable for a kid who started life in a garbage can.

I spoke to Kerrie recently and he said, "Your mom would always focus on 'Okay, how do we do better? How do we make these kids feel loved?' And she didn't do it in an overt way. She went about her business. She didn't look for rewards. She didn't look for anyone to pat her on the back. It all came from her heart. She came in to that center every day, and to her credit it didn't matter if a kid wasn't too bright, or extremely bright, or fat, or thin; she treated us all the same. She had an affection that was genuine. Her point of view was always about teaching, and that's who she was: a teacher."

Yes, my mom worked outside of the public school system. That was her choice. Unlike her, I chose to work within the system, with the simple aim of making public school better for kids. Yet, the question remains: How do we do this?

Lots of well-meaning people have lots of opinions on how to make public schools better: smaller classes, better curriculum, improving as opposed to closing bad schools, giving families vouchers and promoting "school choice," and so on. Some of these are laudable. Some have been tried for decades and have barely nudged the needle. Others have the potential to maim the system so critically that public education could effectively disappear.

What, then, is our best bet to make big improvements at scale? What my mom showed me, and what I've understood intuitively since I was a kid, is that a good teacher is a kid's best bet. While this has been my life's experience, it's important not to be captive to our personal beliefs but to rely on evidence and data. And of late no one has demonstrated the extraordinary impact of teaching more than Raj Chetty, an economist who completely upended the conventional wisdom surrounding the importance of good teaching.

For years, research showed that the gains students got from having a good teacher only lasted so long. Take a third grader who has the good fortune to draw a great teacher. We'll call her Sally. That year Sally learns a lot and does great on her third-grade test, but then she draws mediocre teachers for the next three years. By the end of sixth grade her gains on the tests have evaporated. The fact that Sally once had a great teacher appeared to make no academic difference in her life. That's what many believed.

This changed in late 2014 with the publication of a piece of groundbreaking research. Chetty and his coauthors, John N. Friedman and Jonah E. Rockoff, had taken huge data sets spanning twenty years of historical test scores, and then cross-referenced these with things like earnings and college attendance, to track how students' lives had developed over time. They set out to answer two questions. One: Are standardized test scores a good way to measure teacher quality, even accounting for things like poverty and lack of family support? And two: Do teachers, whether high-quality or not, have a long-term effect on kids' lives? In other words, is Sally, who had an amazing third-grade teacher, doing better in adulthood than her friend Jenny, who had mediocre teachers throughout her young life and who always scored below statewide averages?

Chetty and his coauthors found that the answer to the first question was yes: measuring growth in standardized test scores over time (as opposed to just over the course of one or two years) was a good way to measure whether a teacher was good at teaching. As Chetty said in an extensive interview with the Federal Reserve Bank of Minneapolis, "We basically conclude, first, that value-added measures [like test scores] largely capture the causal effect of teachers rather than differences in the types of students they get. That is, a child who's randomly assigned to a teacher who is high value–added rather than low . . . will end up having higher test scores at the end of the school year." He goes on to say, "Of course, this result only establishes that some teachers are able to raise test scores more effectively than others; it's not clear whether this is driven by teaching to the test or 'deep learning' that has persistent benefits." In a recent conversation I had with Chetty, he also stressed that test scores might not necessarily be the best way to measure teacher quality—other metrics like principal evaluations coupled with test scores might be better—but that they remained very important. "We should use them for what they're worth," he told me, "while trying to improve upon them given what's at stake."

All of this isn't too shocking, and whether it moves you or not probably depends on what you already believe about good teaching and standardized tests. But Chetty circumvents this bias by immediately moving to the second question, which asks whether having a good or, in the language of economists, "high value–added" teacher has lasting benefits.

I'd like to stop for a moment to note how profound and important this question is. For me, the goal has never been just to

raise student test scores or even to increase something as important as high school graduation rates. Those are all means to an
end. The real goal, and one that Chetty tried to address, has always been to transform American lives for the better. That's it.

So, what did he find? Chetty said, "Much to our surprise it
immediately became evident that students who were assigned to
high value–added teachers showed *substantially* larger gains in
terms of earnings, college attendance rates, [and] significantly
lower teenage birth rates; they lived in better neighborhoods as
adults; they had higher levels of retirement savings. Across a broad
spectrum of outcomes, there were *quite* substantial and meaningful impacts on children's long-term success, despite seeing the
fade-out pattern for test scores."

Think about that. This is not about test scores, knowledge, or
even school. It's about *life*. His study showed that the group that
had benefited from having some good teachers had more options,
made better decisions, and had more freedom later in life. Chetty
and his coauthors were able to demonstrate this not in some theo-
retical or anecdotal way but concretely. In one memorable example, they explained that replacing a bad value–added teacher
with a merely average one would increase the lifetime earnings
of a classroom by *$250,000*. His work showed definitively that
teachers matter, and that we have the tools to figure out who and
where the good teachers are.

If we can accept these ideas, and if the political will exists to
make changes, then we can redesign teaching and redefine what it
means to be a teacher in this country. Policies can be enacted that

encourage good teachers to go where they're most needed; we can ask these good teachers what it is they know and how they came to know it; we can continually improve lessons, curriculum, and the tests themselves; and we can help not only kids but also teachers be better learners.

To my mind, what's most lacking in our system is a way for teachers to train and support one another as professionals in the way that doctors and lawyers have for time immemorial. Everyone knows that when a young doctor gets out of medical school she doesn't rush into treating patients by herself: no, she still has years of residency to complete. She may be filled with knowledge, but before she can practice, she needs to go through extensive and comprehensive on-the-job training under the watchful eye of seasoned doctors. The same is true for green lawyers, most of whom don't go right into litigating or negotiating. A lawyer newly minted by his bar exam might clerk for a judge or spend years toiling alongside senior attorneys before being handed the reins in a courtroom or arbitration.

This is not what happens with teachers, who far too often are thrown into classrooms and told to sink or swim. Worse, the vast majority of the schools of education they attended did not give them time in real classrooms working with real groups of diverse learners. A huge 2013 study by the National Council on Teacher Quality found that the majority of newly graduated teachers were not prepared for the classroom at all. The study's introduction starts:

Once the world leader in educational attainment, the United States has slipped well into the middle of the pack. Countries that were considered little more than educational backwaters just a few years ago have leapt to the forefront of student achievement.

There's no shortage of factors for America's educational decline: budget cutbacks, entrenched poverty, crowded classrooms, shorter school years, greater diversity of students than in other countries. The list seems endless. [This] Review has uncovered another cause, one that few would suspect: the colleges and universities producing America's traditionally prepared teachers.

Through an exhaustive and unprecedented examination of how these schools operate, the Review finds they have become an industry of mediocrity, churning out first-year teachers with classroom management skills and content knowledge inadequate to thrive in classrooms.

This study shows that schools of education consistently hurt their students. In the 1970s they made a conscious shift toward "preparing" teachers for their work by putting an emphasis on educational theory instead of "training" them for their job. The ranks of teachers nationwide are getting younger and younger—at the time of the study, first-year teachers taught "around 1.5 million students *every year*, many of whom . . . are already behind in their learning." The authors conclude that our schools of education generally leave "the practice of teaching up to [the] individual discretion" of the new teacher, actively "denying novices access to *what is actually known* about how children learn best."

In fact, nearly two-thirds of all new teachers self-reported that their own educations left them unprepared to stand in front of a class full of kids and teach those kids a lesson. Imagine if two-thirds of our doctors were sent into hospitals unprepared to practice medicine. There would be a revolution. The lie here is that teachers are graduating from school ready for their hugely important job. The truth is that many are not. It's also true that practically no one has their backs. Universities, which frequently treat their schools of education as cash cows, often miseducate teachers; the unions, often more concerned with veteran or re-tired teachers, misrepresent young teachers; and school districts across the country mismanage new teachers by consistently plac-ing them in situations for which they're unprepared.

Imagine a world where all this were different. Imagine if schools of education bucked "the reigning ethos and actually train[ed] their candidates in crucial skills," to quote the same study. Imagine if schools of education were harder to get into, accepting applicants in the top third or quarter of their class, as many high-performing countries do. Imagine if, upon gradua-tion, novice teachers had to do a one- or two-year residency in the classroom of an expert teacher. Imagine if young teachers had the option of signing a higher-risk, higher-reward union contract that would enable them to earn more if they got results with their students (nearly all contracts are currently low-risk, low-reward).

Imagine if teachers could earn two or three times what they now earn, giving them the equivalent pride of other professions like medicine and law. Imagine if teachers were actually valued and not taken for granted. Imagine if we *all* had their backs. Many teachers have the backs of our kids: Why not return the favor?

I firmly believe that if we could come together for the lofty goal of professionalizing teaching, then many positive changes would flow from that. I also think that educational associations, such as teachers' unions, should try to meet these loftier goals and be the engines of this change instead of bulwarks against it.

The other side of the professionalization coin is resources. To be true professionals, teachers don't just need to be more accountable, they need more support—a lot more. They should have better pay, more access to funding for their classrooms, and more respect from political leaders, especially in some Republican-controlled states. For too long these states have starved their systems, preaching that resources don't matter and implying, if not outright stating, that public schools and their teachers don't deserve additional resources. This is a travesty that has gone on for too long. Teachers are right to be furious and demand better, as they currently are in West Virginia, Arizona, Oklahoma, and Kentucky. They are fed up with being shortchanged, underpaid, and feeling like they're being taken advantage of. Teachers should not have to work two jobs to make ends meet. I once met a North Carolina educator who was so desperate she regularly sold her blood plasma to earn a few extra bucks. It's reasonable to ask teachers to work hard, but it is not reasonable to ask them to take these kinds of desperate measures.

who have a bachelor's degree enjoy the country's highest average starting salary, at nearly $59,000 per year, which is significant considering that the average salary of veteran teachers nationwide is about $58,000 per year—a figure that's one percent *lower* in inflation-adjusted dollars than the average 1991 teacher salary!) The list goes on, from Louisiana to Colorado and many places in between, but these remain outliers in the context of the 14,000 district–100,000 school–50 million student–$650 billion system that is American K–12 public education.

In an earlier chapter I told a story about attending a meeting in Chicago with concerned parents over the imminent closing of their children's school. One of those parents accused me of being racist, to which I replied that if I were racist, then I'd leave everything exactly as it was. Their child's school would stay open and their kids would continue to be warehoused and subjected to social promotion. That school would do nothing to better educate their children, and it would all but guarantee that their kids would have no chance at breaking their personal cycle of poverty. This same logic applies to teachers. If I didn't care about teachers, then I wouldn't challenge the current system. I wouldn't mind if they didn't professionalize. I'd say, *Keep showing up, keep flogging away, keep battling every day without the mentoring, resources, or support that you need to truly be your best. You're on your own.*

The lie underneath all of this is one that says America values its teachers. But the truth is we don't. If we really valued the women and men dedicated to educating our children, then our teachers would be more respected, better paid, and have tons of

"WE MATTER!"

For evidence of this, we need look no further than the debate surrounding gun control in America.

In April 2009, only a few months after being sworn in as secretary of education, I was stunned to find myself featured on the cover of a magazine I'd never heard of called *America's 1st Freedom*. I quickly learned this was a National Rifle Association publication, and the article, which has since been scrubbed from the Internet as if it never existed, was titled, "Arne Duncan: Education at the Extremez." Its author, with whom I'd never spoken, claimed I was "the most extreme anti-gun member of President Obama's Cabinet."

I can't speak for other secretaries, but it is true that I have no love for guns. During the 2007–2008 school year, my last at Chicago Public Schools, we lost thirty-four school-aged kids to gun violence. Our schools were safe—school was often the safest part of a child's day—but we couldn't protect them once they left the building, and during my more than seven years as CEO of CPS we lost one child every two or three weeks. Their memorials were far and away the most scarring aspect of the job. Each was harder to go to than the last.

Harder still was meeting the families and friends of these victims. It was unbearable to sit in living rooms with loved ones, holding photographs of the child who'd brought us together but whom I'd never meet. Likewise, it was almost impossible not to fall apart when I sat in classes full of children while trying and often failing to make sense of the senseless. Their pain, fear, anger, and heartbreak are hard to articulate. So is their level of trauma. When I visit Chicago schools now I ask everyone who has been touched by gun violence to raise their hands. Every time nearly every hand goes up, and often they all go up. This is true of grade schoolers, middle schoolers, and high schoolers all across the South and West Sides. A brother shot, an aunt, a parent, a friend, sometimes even the students themselves. Not all die, but all are changed. The level of fear that our kids live with every single day is extraordinary. Throughout my life I've preached to children: "Think long term," and "Think about college." But if a kid is just trying to survive every day, then that stuff is like a foreign language. It doesn't quite make sense.

Our kids who live like this know that on any given day it can be them, and they know that, on many levels, they've been robbed of their childhoods. The overwhelming majority of these young victims aren't involved in gangs or drugs; they're just kids. In Chicago, what sentences them to death is often nothing more than a combination of socioeconomics and bad luck.

Starkesia Reed had the bad luck to be getting ready for school in her living room one morning. An honor roll ninth grader at Harper High School, Starkesia lived in Englewood, one of Chicago's toughest neighborhoods. Her family was big—eleven kids—with a mom and a dad who each had decent working-class jobs. They were a strong family that was doing everything right, but it didn't matter. On the morning of March 3, 2006, Starkesia heard some loud noises outside her wood-frame house and went to the window to investigate. While standing there, a high-caliber bullet, aimlessly sprayed from an AK-47, tore through her window and struck her in the eye. The glass didn't shatter, but she died instantly. Her murderer was eventually caught and convicted, and is currently serving a 150-year sentence.

Terrell Bosley had the bad luck to be in the Lights of Zion Ministries church parking lot in West Pullman. He was eighteen, an accomplished bass player, and a fixture in church choirs and bands across the South Side. He'd graduated from high school and was taking classes at a local community college. He was a good kid with two little brothers. His parents, Pam and Tom, had a great marriage and were solidly middle-class. None of that mattered. On April 4, 2006, Terrell died because he was carrying a drum kit into the church when a man drove up and opened fire for no reason. One of Terrell's friends was also struck in the hip and thigh, but he survived. Terrell's case remains unsolved.

Blair Holt, sixteen, had the bad luck to be riding a packed Chicago Transit Authority bus on May 7, 2007. At a busy stop another teenager, fifteen, stepped onto the bus. His friend, seventeen, passed him a loaded 9-millimeter pistol and the fifteen-year-old opened fire. The surveillance video showed a bus full of teens and children going home after-school. The target was unclear, but the shooting was gang-related and Blair wasn't their intended victim. He was a good student at Julian High, the only child of Ron Holt, a long-serving Chicago cop who'd worked with the gang crimes unit, and Annette Nance-Holt, a battalion chief in the Chicago Fire Department. None of this mattered. As the shooter opened fire, Blair pushed a friend to the ground and smothered her. He was struck in the torso and died shortly afterward. His friend was unharmed. Against the odds, his murderer was caught and is now serving a seventy-five-year sentence; the kid who passed him the gun got ten.

(It's worth noting that, as recent as 2017, about 82 percent of Chicago gun deaths go unsolved, along with about 95 percent of nonfatal shootings. In other words, if you want to shoot, you're all but guaranteed to get away with it. It's also worth noting that while Chicago's gun laws are strict, Starkesia's murderer was able to buy his AK-47, along with two handguns, at an Indiana gun shop using a fake ID. He would have been ineligible to get these weapons in Indiana if he'd used his real ID, since he was under investigation for armed robbery.)

I met each of the kids' families in the immediate aftermath of their deaths. It's strange the things we remember. When I went to Starkesia's house, I sat in the living room where she died. One of her older brothers had knocked away the pane of glass that the bullet had passed through and perched a stuffed Minnie Mouse in its place. Their leather couch was worn and patched across one cushion with a single strip of tape. The tape felt like a perfect metaphor for a working-class family just managing to hold things together. Along with the Minnie Mouse doll and the pointless horror of Starkesia's murder, it was a picture of grief that I've not been able to forget or shake.

These things completely change a person. Starkesia's mom, Denise, knows this, and Blair and Terrell's mothers, Annette and Pam, know it too. Pam tried to commit suicide not once but twice. Today, Pam and Annette work together for their organization Purpose Over Pain, which gives support to grieving families, fights for gun control laws, and attempts to steer young people away from violence in the first place.

I currently work for an organization called Creating Real Economic Destiny, or Chicago CRED, that's trying to change the economic landscape on the South and West Sides by working directly with young men who are most at risk of shooting or being shot. Through this work, I still regularly see Pam and Annette. Whenever I ask what they need most, they give two answers. First, they want more support and counseling for parents who've lost children. "There are just so many, Arne," Pam recently told me. Second, they want jobs for the forgotten young people of Chicago, especially young black men like the ones I work with at CRED. Pam and Annette also say that their young people need better schools and teachers. They need opportunities. They need nonviolent infractions like shoplifting or trespassing—even low-level drug dealing—expunged from their records. There are too many young men out there with minor marks on their record that effectively disqualify them from employment, which just forces them back to the street to make money.

A lot of people who don't live or work in these communities wonder why these young men wind up on the street in the first place. Often their reasons are perfectly rational. I've heard the stories a thousand times: Mom's at home crying every night, little sisters and brothers are hungry, the family needs new shoes and pencils for school, bills need to be paid, diapers need to be bought. And on and on. There are hardly any legit jobs available in their community, so what can a kid do—this little man of the house, usually only fourteen or fifteen years old? *What can he do?* He can go down and talk to the guy on the corner. When the rest of us—in our "good" homes, in our suburbs, in our office jobs—are absent, these guys are ever-present. The guy on the corner is *always* there and he's *always* hiring—rain, snow, sleet, or sweltering sun. The vast majority of these kids aren't bad, they're just desperate. Think about it: What would you do? Forget whether it's legal, or right, or dangerous: asking the guy on the corner for work is the most rational thing they *can* do, because more often than not it's their only viable option to earn some money. That our society accepts this, and does so little to offer better options, should be a huge source of civic shame. Yet it isn't.

In spite of all these troubles in Chicago, the more time I spent in DC, the more wistful I became for my hometown. Cabinet-level jobs aren't lonely, but on most days I flew along at 30,000 feet. Yes, I had the back-to-school bus tours every year, and, yes, I made a point to visit every single state in the union, but it was difficult to build lasting connections. I visited hundreds of public schools while I was education secretary, but I visited only about a dozen more than once. I suppose this is a price one pays for wanting to make big changes to the status quo, but I missed the chance to build relationships. I missed school functions, visiting churches on the weekend, going to games, and being a part of a single system—even one as lopsided and challenging as Chicago's. I craved those connections, and I knew pretty early on that when my time was done in DC, I'd return home.

The things I did *not* miss, however, were the visits to these families and the funerals. DC granted me an unexpected emotional reprieve, and it took a while for me to appreciate this and not feel guilty about it. Things weren't any better in Chicago—in fact, between 2009 and the present the violence has gotten much, much worse—but I'd be lying if I said I missed going to funerals. Over seven years in DC I attended a total of three services—about a month's worth in Chicago. Two of those were back home for children whose deaths were so senseless that I felt I needed to pay my respects.

I traveled with First Lady Michelle Obama and Valerie Jarrett to the service of Hadiya Pendleton, an honor roll student who'd been hit by a stray bullet while on a swing set only a couple of blocks from my mom's center. The other was for Tyshawn Lee. He'd been killed assassination-style by gang members to punish Tyshawn's father for some unknown transgression. Tyshawn's murder violated all the rules of the street, and even by Chicago standards it felt significant. His father was at the service, where I shook his hand and put my arm around him. Just seeing him in the pews—a man who knew his son was dead because of him—was an image I'll never forget.

However, the third funeral had nothing to do with Chicago. It wasn't for a child. It was for the principal of Sandy Hook Elementary School, Dawn Hochsprung, aged forty-seven.

I don't remember much about the specifics of what happened on December 14, 2012. The shock of what our country learned that morning was too great. What I can recall is that, not long after arriving at work, Joanne rushed into my office and said, "Arne, come with me." I could tell right away that it wasn't good.

It was a gray and cold day, befitting the news that Joanne and I watched with a small number of staff. Many cried. Some left the room. I spoke with Connecticut's chief education officer, who was en route to the scene. All I remember him saying was, "This is bad, Arne. This is really, really bad." The hushed tone of his voice said more than his words. I remember canceling that day's schedule, and the next day's as well, and convening a meeting in my office. We sat there dumbstruck, but then we went around the table. Some of us told stories, which was out of the ordinary. Normally we were all business, very workaday, and our plates were so full that we didn't have time for stories.

But that day time stopped. One man—a brilliant teacher and former union president from Denver named Brad Jupp—told us about his schizophrenic brother, Neil. "He grew to adulthood, but his life was hard. . . . He died ten years ago. I miss him all the time." Brad wouldn't say how or why Neil had died, but then he emphatically said, "Muddying the waters with mental health isn't going to do anyone any good." We didn't know anything about the Sandy Hook shooter at that point, but it was a safe bet that the issue of mental health would come up as a way to both explain what had happened and to avoid doing anything about enacting sensible gun control laws.

Brad continued, "This is a gun problem, not a mental health problem. Mental illness can become a vehicle to mass violence *only* in the presence of guns."

I couldn't have agreed more. America isn't the only country with mental health issues, or violent video games, or single-parent families, to name but a few favorite scapegoats of gun control opponents. However, we are the only country in the world with hundreds of millions of guns available for practically anyone to purchase or use.

As we sat at that table we decided that, as long as the president could sustain it, we would do whatever we could to push for new gun laws. We believed that if the Sandy Hook shooter hadn't had access to a Bushmaster assault rifle and a pair of semiautomatic handguns, then he would never have been able to do what he did that day. He would not have killed Dawn Hochsprung. Or his own mother, who supplied him with the guns. Or the five other women who worked at Sandy Hook Elementary. Or the twenty innocent first graders, all aged six or seven.

The shooting took place on a Friday. President Obama traveled to Newtown on Sunday, and I went the following Wednesday to meet families, students, and teachers. I traveled with Vice President Joe Biden, who also wanted to pay his respects and do whatever he could to help the families heal. It was December 19, only one day after the fortieth anniversary of the tragic death of his first wife and daughter in a car accident on December 18, 1972. I didn't know Joe Biden before going to DC, but I was lucky enough to get to know him well, and our friendship grew that much stronger after Newtown. The trip was overwhelming in every way, but I remember being taken to a large meeting area, maybe at a church or at another nearby school, and making my way through the room. I spoke with parents and teachers, held children, got down on a knee to talk to siblings of the deceased. There were a lot of tears but also smiles. I remember looking across the room at one point and just watching the vice president for a minute. I'd been to more funerals than I could count, and had known so many who'd been killed, but these experiences weren't deeply personal for me in the way this one was for Vice President Biden. He intimately knew this level of grief, a knowledge I simply lacked. He was familiar with the sadness, the rage, and the confusion of losing a child and spouse. He knew what it was like to feel, as he wrote in his book *Promises to Keep*, as though "God had played a horrible trick on me." He could bring all of his experience to bear on helping the families impacted by this unspeakable tragedy as they began the long path toward healing.

The Sandy Hook Massacre took five minutes and three seconds. During that time, 154 rounds of ammunition left the gunman's weapons. I wish I could say those five minutes and three seconds changed America, but as we know, they didn't. For many years nothing changed. Charleston happened—9 killed and one injured at a church service. Orlando happened—49 killed (not counting the gunman) and 53 injured at a nightclub. Las Vegas happened—the worst mass shooting in the nation's history—58 killed (not counting the gunman) and 422 injured by gunfire at an outdoor concert. This man-made disaster we've created and allowed to fester torments and terrorizes our children. At the time of writing and since 2009, there have been 288 school shootings in the United States. The country with the second most is Mexico—with *eight*. India, which has four times as many people as the United States, has had five. Canada has had two. This situation is unacceptable. Other nations make other choices, and their citizens are safer as a result. Think of the gift these countries have given their sons and daughters. Think of what these countries are saying to their teachers: *We already ask enough of you, so you concentrate on doing your very hard job and we'll do the job of keeping you and your students safe.* The students in these other countries don't have to do active shooter drills at school. They don't have to say to the post-shooting news cameras, as Paige Curry, a seventeen-year-old at Santa Fe High School in Texas, said with a shrug, "I've always kind of thought it was going to happen here, too." Why do we ask our children and our citizens to go to school or to church or to a nightclub or to a concert, thinking *This could be the last day of my life because someone might show up with an assault rifle?*

Before Newtown, I believed it would take the deaths of young white kids to force people to act. Somehow Columbine was exempt—maybe because it feels like the first modern American school massacre, or maybe because the victims weren't first graders. I'm not proud of this belief, but it's what I thought. I knew from experience that our society didn't value black and brown lives the same way it valued white lives. I knew it from Sue's center and my time at CPS. I knew it from my own friends who were killed when I was a teenager playing ball all over the South and West Sides. I lost good friends, mentors, and guys who protected me. Young men like Little Danny Sardin, Tredarryl Fort, LuVertus Hardy.

Unfortunately, after Newtown, our lack of empathy and our inability to do what was right was completely exposed. These were babies who'd been executed in their classroom. When the dust settled, we chose to protect our guns, not our kids. We chose metal over flesh. This too should have been a massive source of civic shame, but somehow it wasn't. Somehow, keeping and even expanding access to guns, as happened throughout the Obama presidency, became more necessary after the massacre. Somehow, the sacrifice of our children was an acceptable price to pay for our freedom, however it is you want to define that.

After Newtown, the NRA had the power to immediately shift the debate to mentally ill shooters and the constitutional rights of law-abiding gun owners, which I'm not interested in doing away with. By the way, you'll notice that when black and brown kids get killed by the hundreds, as they have been in Chicago and other cities for years and years, the NRA doesn't talk about mental illness. Instead, when black and brown kids get slaughtered the NRA and its sympathizers more often talk about law and order, policing, broken families, drugs, gangs—anything but the easy availability of guns as protected by the National Rifle Association and the politicians beholden to it.

When black and brown kids go down in droves, the implication is not that a single person is defective, as with the Sandy Hook killer, but instead that an entire population is defective. As if people of color are somehow prone to violence. As if Starkesia, Blair, Terrell, Hadiya, and Tyshawn—and countless others like them—deserved to die in her living room, on his bus ride home from school, walking into his church, as she sat on the swings, or on his knees with a gun to the back of his head.

The lives of black and brown Americans are absolutely and systemically less valued than those of white Americans, but Newtown showed that, in truth, we don't value the lives of our young people at all. It exposed so much hypocrisy, so much mendacity.

All that mattered to the NRA and those loyal to it was the unfettered right for any American to buy any type of firearm and have the freedom to carry that firearm anywhere they wanted to. This was the way it was for many years after that unspeakable and fully preventable tragedy, and this was the way the NRA always wants it to be.

But then, as I finished writing this book, something tragic yet remarkable happened. On February 14, 2018, a very troubled young man walked into a high school in Parkland, Florida, and murdered seventeen people and wounded sixteen others, most of them students. Somehow, against the odds, this tragedy has changed the conversation. For the first time, the teens directly impacted by this violence are leading.

After Parkland, the NRA was unable to shift the debate to mental illness or school safety. After Parkland, students spoke up, which wasn't possible after Newtown. After Parkland, the most vocal constituency was not the gun lobby and its servants but young people who are fed up with active shooter drills and constant, simmering fear. After Parkland, the issue of gun control survived many news cycles through the force of will, eloquence, and conviction of those most touched by what happened there: young survivors.

The activists from Marjory Stoneman Douglas High School—Emma González, David Hogg, Jaclyn Corin, Alex Wind, Cameron Kasky, Samuel Zeif, plus many, many more—have, in some ways, been preparing for this their entire lives. While they haven't lived with the level of trauma experienced by the youth of Chicago, they have grown up knowing that, however remote, there was a chance that their school could be the next to suffer from our distinctly American brand of gun violence.

You may wonder what the shooting at Stoneman Douglas, a public high school that serves a student body that's pretty affluent, has to do with the violence afflicting poor black and brown kids all over Chicago?

To answer that, I'd like to tell you about a school named North Lawndale College Prep and one of its students, a young man named D'Angelo McDade. D'Angelo recently joined forces with Emma González, and students at North Lawndale have formed a tight if unlikely bond with the Parkland students.

D'Angelo's story started years earlier, before he was even born, when I was still new to Chicago Public Schools. In 1998, I helped with the formation of North Lawndale College Prep, a new charter high school on the West Side. One of the school's founders, a former priest named John Horan, who would serve as dean of students for years, had previously worked for the "I Have a Dream" Foundation in Chicago. Our lives had intersected many times and I knew John well. He understood the amount of work it took to change the lives of young, traumatized people, and he knew that with effort and goodwill it could be done.

Several years after North Lawndale's founding, when D'Angelo was a young grade schooler and I was CEO, John called me with a strange request. His school, whose entryways were guarded by metal detectors, had recently been allocated money for eight or nine additional school resource officers, aka security guards. But he wanted something else. "I'd like to take that money and hire eight or nine school counselors instead, Arne," he said.

"Really?"

"Yes. We have a science teacher here named Tiffany Childress, and she's been doing a lot of Kingian Nonviolence work with the students. It's just beginning to take root and they need support. It's student-centered and I think they have a shot at making a difference. They're calling themselves 'Peace Warriors.'"

It was a brilliant idea that I hadn't been smart enough to think of myself: counselors instead of guards. Support instead of policing. In their daily lives, Chicago kids got very little of the former, while the latter was always just around the corner. John promised that if the idea didn't bear fruit, then we could revisit what to do with the funding, so I gave the go-ahead. But if it *did* work, then North Lawndale could serve as a model for other schools.

This was particularly important to me at the time because the truth was that we had a problem with juvenile arrests in Chicago. The basic issue was that there were too many. We'd asked the police superintendent, Phil Cline, and his team to look into the data and to challenge his officers on how many school-age kids they arrested. What they came back with floored me.

The Chicago police operated on three shifts: 8:00 a.m. to 4:00 p.m., 4:00 p.m. to 12:00 a.m., and 12:00 a.m. to 8:00 a.m. I expected most of their juvenile arrests to occur on the 4:00 p.m to 12:00 a.m. shift, since that included the after-school hours when kids are running around with time on their hands. Instead, when Superintendent Cline got back to me he said that the majority of kids were getting arrested during the 8:00 a.m. to 4:00 p.m. shift. Meaning, *they were being arrested while they were in school.* The police hadn't created this problem. People working at CPS had.

We'd met the enemy, and it was us.

We looked into it and quickly discovered that schools usually called the cops because they couldn't deal with a student who was acting out, sometimes violently but more often not. About 60 percent of the arrests came from only about 15 percent of schools. Surprisingly, some schools serving the exact same type of students had no issues, while another school only a few blocks away practically had a hotline to the local precinct. In other words, separate schools faced similar challenges, but these were handled very differently.

To fix this, we went to the trouble spots and rolled up our sleeves. We did retraining and conflict resolution and deescalation work. We weren't being soft on crime—if a kid brought a gun or knife to school, the cops got called—but we did give everyone better intervention tools. Instead of shoving a kid into a squad car, we'd try to get his school to ask him, "Why are you so angry today?" He might not answer right away, but if they could build trust they'd get there. Eventually he'd say something like, "Mom got beat up last night," or "A friend got shot," or "I couldn't sleep because we have no heat and it's twenty degrees outside." That's real-life stuff. Those *are* things to be angry about.

So when John called and told me about his Peace Warriors, I was doubly intrigued. As he explained it, the students would primarily be responsible for resolving conflicts and accountable for their behavior and the behavior of their peers. They would aspire to practice the Golden Rule, to learn not to retaliate, and to subscribe to the idea that they should be the change that they want to see in the world. They would try to love their enemies and ultimately turn them into friends. Peace was literally their goal. On average, North Lawndale dealt with non-gun-related violence two or three times a week, and it affected everyone. But to learn how to do all of this work, the students and faculty needed extra support. That's where the counselors came in.

Long story short, it worked amazingly well. The school graded itself on peace, as measured by the number of violent altercations, and within only a couple years they consistently got an A, eventually reaching fewer than ten incidents per year as opposed to ten per month. The world outside the school was still dangerous, and its students were still getting shot at, but inside they were safe and making a difference. Suspensions and expulsions plummeted, and grades and test scores improved. (The decline in suspensions was so dramatic that the data crunchers at CPS once sent a team of disbelieving monitors to North Lawndale to ensure that John and his team weren't cooking the books.) Everyone bought in and the metal detectors came down. They proved that their students didn't need more policing, they needed more care.

(Sadly, after a round of recent statewide budget cuts that trimmed North Lawndale's staff by 20 percent, the metal detectors went back up. This is less a reflection on the school, which continues to be successful with its peace work, than a reflection on the community at large, which has only gotten more and more dangerous over the last decade, in part because of the easy availability of guns in neighboring states like Indiana.)

This brings me back to D'Angelo McDade, one of North Lawndale's current Peace Warriors. I met D'Angelo in early 2017 through Chicago CRED and was stunned to learn that he and a few of his friends were voluntarily going into elementary schools to teach younger kids about peace and conflict resolution. He was barely seventeen years old but he had a preacher's demeanor in a linebacker's body. Not long after we met, D'Angelo sat on his grandfather's porch with his cousin and his grandpa. As they chatted, a car drove by and sprayed the neighborhood with bullets, attempting to hit rival gang members. D'Angelo wasn't the target but he was struck. Luckily, he survived, but he still carries a bullet in his leg.

That spring, I talked to D'Angelo about using his volunteer work as the inspiration for a summer jobs program for like-minded teens across the city. We would pay young people to teach members of the community how to solve conflicts nonviolently, and to create peace projects in their neighborhoods. D'Angelo and his friends agreed, and during the summer of 2017 we employed 1,100 young men and women across the South and West Sides. It was so successful that we're planning on employing 1,400 over the summer of 2018.

After Parkland, I helped coordinate a series of meetings between the young Florida and Chicago activists. While nearly everyone I knew in Chicago was excited that a meaningful gun violence discussion had sprung up around the Parkland students, there was some resentment that cut right to the core of America's racial divide. Black and brown kids died all the time in Chicago and elsewhere, and no one seemed to care; but when a group of vocal and well-spoken middle-class white kids were the victims, the world was appalled. It was completely unfair. But D'Angelo, perhaps because of the work he'd been doing, didn't see it this way. "It was never a feeling of jealousy," he said. "It was a feeling of 'We can leverage this.'"

The weekend before the nationwide school walkouts in March 2018, we organized a trip that flew D'Angelo and half a dozen other young Chicagoans down to Parkland to stay with Emma González at her home. For nearly all of our kids, this was the first time they'd been on an airplane. Some had never left Chicago before. As they cruised around Florida, where it was as warm as Chicago in the summertime, they learned that a lot of people had their own swimming pools, and that "gated communities" were not places that housed convicted criminals. I wasn't there, but I have some video and I've spoken with D'Angelo and some of the other activists. From word one, Emma put the issue of white privilege on the table, acknowledging that while they were getting most of the media attention, what had happened was something that had happened to all of them. As Emma wrote in a piece for *Harper's Bazaar*, "Who are we? We are the people who died in the freshman building on Valentine's Day at Douglas High, and the people who died in every mass shooting in U.S. history. We are everyone who has been shot at, grazed or pierced by bullets, terrorized by the presence of guns and gun violence in America.

We are kids, we are parents, we are students, we are teachers. We are tired of practicing school shooter drills and feeling scared of something we should never have to think about. We are tired of being ignored. So we are speaking up for those who don't have anyone listening to them, for those who can't talk about it just yet, and for those who will never speak again. We are grieving, we are furious, and we are using our words fiercely and desperately because that's the only thing standing between us and this happening again."

The two groups met on her screened-in back porch next to her swimming pool. Emma asked what it was like for D'Angelo and his friends to live the way they did. If they were going to speak out against gun violence together, then she wanted permission to speak out against the violence suffered by everyone, not just the victims at her school. Would they give it to her?

Yes.

In one memorable moment, D'Angelo, then eighteen, said, "[That] day has now turned into your reality. And your reality has turned into your life's work. What I hear is—allow us who are sitting here to work as cohorts. As your Chicago team, as your Florida team. A team to build this [into] what it needs to be.

"But—and this is my 'but.'" He turned to Emma and waved an index finger, not to scold but to hammer home his question: "Can you give us the authority to accept this suffering? Can you give us the authority to achieve this goal with you? That's what we're sitting here at this table to discuss. We can't just sit and say, 'Hey, we're going to take on this mission and run with it without your blessing or without your support.' Because you are the founders. You have the platform. We're just here to move you further. Who will help you get to your place? Who will help us get to our place?"

No one answered those last two questions, because no one had to. These were black kids and white kids, poorer kids and kids with their own swimming pools, urban kids and suburban kids, coming together to ask permission to help one another. Sit with that.

Late that Saturday night, the "Chicago cohort" flew home. John Horan picked up D'Angelo and another Peace Warrior, Alex King, at O'Hare. He drove them home, and they talked about what had happened, but before they even got to their destinations the real world came rushing back on them. John was going to pull over at a gas station on the West Side but didn't because it was surrounded by police, their cars' cherry lights twirling, their guns drawn. Young black men lay prone on the dirty, pungent ground around the pumps, their hands on the backs of their heads. No shots had been fired, but John, D'Angelo, and Alex didn't hang around to find out if any would be.

In the middle of that week, during the nationwide school walkout, D'Angelo led a group of hundreds of Chicago students, nearly all of them black, in protest against gun violence and in favor of stricter gun laws. They each wore black and had a red strip of tape over their lips, each bearing a message. D'Angelo's read, "WE MATTER!" The seventeen students at the front of his group each carried a large purple cross that they'd made out of nailed-together two-by-fours. Each cross bore a framed picture of one of the Parkland victims, nearly all of them white.

Two weekends later, the Parkland students came to Chicago to meet D'Angelo and his friends on their home turf. They met at Saint Sabina Church, where Father Mike Pfleger has worked in the community and against the scourge of gun violence for decades, and strategized for the March for Our Lives on March 24, 2018, in DC. For some of the Florida kids it was the first time they'd been to a place where it got cold in the wintertime. New experiences cut both ways.

Then, a week later, they reconvened in Washington for the March. Emma and the other Parkland students rightly got a ton of press, but there were many speakers that day from across the country. Two of them were D'Angelo and Alex King. They walked onto the stage together in bright blue hoodies, tape again covering their mouths. Alex removed his and spoke first. He'd lost his nephew in May 2017, only two weeks after his sixteenth birthday. Alex has told me that he knows more than fifty people who have been shot. D'Angelo reached out and rubbed his friend's shoulders as Alex repeatedly called everyone assembled "family." He said, "Our pain makes us family. Our hurt brings us closer together." At the close of his speech he led the crowd in a "unity clap" they do at North Lawndale and invoked Dr. Martin Luther King Jr.'s "beloved community," asking everyone to make change together.

D'Angelo removed the tape from his lips and opened with the same clap. Then he spoke. He was fiery and direct. "We are survivors," he said. "We are survivors of a cruel and silent nation, where freedom, justice, equality, and purpose are not upheld. . . . When will we understand that nonviolence is the way of life for a courageous people?" I was in the crowd with my family and four hundred young Chicagoans who Chicago CRED had bused to DC. I teared up a lot that day, and I definitely cried when he said, "I stand before you representing the body of those who've lost their lives to gun violence." I thought of so many people, but especially of Starkesia, Terrell, and Blair. D'Angelo continued, talking about the ideal and the work of peace, and also invoking Dr. King: "Darkness cannot drive out darkness, only light can do that. Hate cannot drive out hate, only love can do that. Violence cannot drive out violence, only peace can do that! . . . Youth must now be the change that we seek!" I cheered and could not have agreed more.

At some point during these busy days I was interviewed by a local Chicago TV station about all of the work these young people were doing. The interviewer asked how it was that I and people like me were leading them. I interrupted her: "No, I'm not leading. I'm following. The students are the leaders, and I'm following them. I'm doing whatever I can to help them, but that's it."

For some reason the NRA singled me out back in 2009—probably because for a long time I'd been begging for the things that Emma and D'Angelo were now demanding. Over the past four decades I've known so many people lost to senseless gun violence that I can no longer count them. This isn't the world we're supposed to live in. This isn't the world children—black, brown, white, poor, rich, urban, rural, however you want to slice it—deserve. If they can do the work that adults have been unable or unwilling to do, then I am beyond happy to follow them to the ends of the earth.

These are American students from opposite ends of the educational spectrum. If I played even a minuscule part in the development of these leaders and the leaders that will spring up around them, then I can say that a life spent in the field of education has been well worth it. They have restored the hope that was stripped from me by Newtown. Whether they succeed tomorrow or ten years from now, I believe that they can force this country to stop lying to itself and to truly value our children, our teachers, and, I hope one day, our amazing public schools. It's obvious that students need teachers, but what I am learning from them is that teachers also need students.

I am prouder of them than words can express.

HOW SCHOOLS
WORK

I'd like to close this book about education in a place that too
often, and inexplicably, fades into the background of many
conversations about education: a classroom.

The classroom in question is an eighth-grade English class,
taught by Ms. Malagic at the Lewis School of Excellence, a PK–8
Chicago public school in the West Side neighborhood of North
Austin. The Lewis School is one of thirty-one Chicago schools
managed by the Academy for Urban School Leadership. AUSL
is not a charter network but rather a nonprofit organization
that serves regular public schools and whose mission is to create "schools of excellence by developing highly effective teachers
and transforming educational outcomes for students in the lowest

performing schools." AUSL grew out of a teacher residency program that was the brainchild of my good friend Mike Koldyke, a businessman and philanthropist committed to improving public education. Since then, the organization has flourished, transforming the lives of thousands of students, parents, and teachers.

The students I sat with on the day of my visit were going over an upcoming essay assignment based on their reading of William Shakespeare's *A Midsummer Night's Dream*. Ms. Malagic—who is white, wears glasses, and has a light midwestern accent—asked each student to pick a character and then write a "confessional" from that character's perspective. My memory of *A Midsummer Night's Dream* is sketchy, but the main theme Ms. Malagic's class was exploring concerned control in the fairy kingdom: How did their character control another character? Why did they want to control that character? And what was the result of their attempts at control?

I sat along the back wall next to an empty desk with a sign over it that read "Zen Space." It was later explained to me that this was where a kid could go to sit and be alone. No one would talk to him, no one would ask him to do anything. Sometimes students went there to calm down, other times to forget about whatever it was that was bothering them outside of school. It was a space to get re-centered on learning.

There were about twenty students, all of them black or Latino, and all sitting at long shared desks, facing the front of the room. The overheads were off: the only light came from the gray winter sky outside and the glow of the projector in the middle aisle, which displayed a sample essay on the Smart Board behind Ms. Malagic. She and the students took turns reading it. The essay was from Puck's perspective. It was an entertaining story written in modern (as opposed to Shakespearean) English about why Puck enjoyed being a prankster and the mischief he got into as a result. About half the students took turns reading, and none of them expressed any trepidation about doing so, although the teacher was the most entertaining reader of them all. She took a lot of joy in acting and also in modeling what a good speaker sounded like.

Ms. Malagic paused to give the kids a quick in-class assignment, asking them to identify the kinds of things the author had done to make the piece well written. They worked among themselves for a few minutes, talking back and forth in small groups. When Ms. Malagic quieted the room and called on them, they cited the use of details, specific references to the text, the way the author used Puck's point of view, and the fact that the author answered all of the assignment's questions: how, why, and to what end Puck had attempted to control other characters in the play. One student added that the author must have proofread their work.

They continued reading the sample. Ms. Malagic gently reminded students now and then to "track," or make eye contact, with the speaker, whether it was her or another student, and only once did she have to correct a student's behavior—which was for what she perceived as reading without bothering to pay attention to the words, not anything disruptive. At one point a clear-voiced girl named Pamela paused in mid-sentence. Ms. Malagic said, "You can say it." Pamela continued, starting with the word "ass." The class giggled. Every student was into it, and the boys spoke as much and as freely as the girls. No less than ten times did the class respond with finger snaps of support, and when someone said something especially insightful, Ms. Malagic gave that student points on a merit chart she projected on the Smart Board. Each student had an emoji-like avatar with a number below it: this was the running total of points each student got. Eventually, awards would be given on student-, class-, grade-, and school-wide levels for meeting goals. The principal, Aquabah Gonney-Buckner, told me later that the eighth grade was currently competing for a Valentine's Day dance.

The lesson continued. A disagreement broke out between a boy and girl over Puck's motivation for controlling Lysander. Ms. Malagic said, "All right—that's a good thing, to disagree!" A few minutes later a boy up front said, "I have a compliment." Snaps went around the room as if they were saying, *Let's hear it!* Ms. Malagic said, "A compliment! Go." The boy said he liked the way that one of the students who'd disagreed had reasoned through her answer. Ms. Malagic gave him points for his compliment and gave the girl points for clarity. Before Ms. Malagic could resume the lesson, another boy—a big kid who looked more like a football player than someone who'd dig Shakespeare—said, "I have a compliment too." More snaps. "Go on, Richard," Ms. Malagic said. "I just wanted to say I thought it was cool that you guys disagreed and didn't bug out or get into any kind of an argument.

You didn't think the same thing, but you didn't take it personally and I think that's really nice." Ms. Malagic drove it home by adding, "It's also nice that you noticed that, Richard. It makes other students feel appreciated that you're listening to them. It encourages them to want to speak."

I've been in lots of classrooms over the years and I've seen this kind of thing play out more times than I can count, but this classroom struck me. There was no lag; everyone was on. The teacher wasn't lecturing her kids and asking a few star pupils here and there for answers; they were having a conversation, and getting somewhere with it. I doubt everyone in that room was friends with everyone else, but they were all respectful, into the material, and completely engaged. Think about a room full of eighth graders anywhere; forget that these were almost all kids who came from poor homes in a neighborhood that sometimes felt more like a war zone than a community. Would you expect to see this level of interest in a typical eighth-grade English class? I doubt it.

(And it was not because I was there. The principal and I dropped in after they'd started and they didn't know who I was until after I left. Besides, these kids were used to other teachers, observers, and the principal sitting in on their classwork. That's the AUSL way.)

What Ms. Malagic, who came off as much a mentor and friend as she did a teacher, was able to share with her kids was remarkable. I had no doubt that when they sat down that night at home to write their own essays, they'd have the confidence to do it to the best of their ability and also not be afraid to take chances, or even fail, if that's what happened. They'd find a way to work through it together.

I left the classroom before they finished, everyone quietly thanking me before continuing. Mrs. Gonney-Buckner and I made our way through the halls toward her office. Lewis had been an AUSL school for about three and a half years and it was still in the process of turning around. It had been a bad school before: Mrs. Gonney-Buckner had parents who'd gone to Lewis and who told her stories about how kids fought all the time, throwing chairs all over the place, even out the windows. Chicago schools all have a public grade—3, 2, 2+, 1, or 1+, with 1+ being the best—and Lewis was a middle-of-the-pack 2+, but it was on its way.

I asked her about the eighth graders who'd been there before AUSL. "What's the difference for them?"

"The difference is the level of education," she said as she pushed through a set of metal double doors and led me downstairs. "The work they do is intense and intentional. Before, they wouldn't have had access to Shakespeare; and if they did, they might not have cared about it. They know that if they put in the work, then they'll leave here prepared for high school. They know what it was like before, and they know that they have something special here now. They don't take it for granted. That's one reason they were so into that class and Ms. Malagic. They know that all of the adults in this building are accountable to themselves and to their students. For the students that adds a level of 'I've gotta get this together. I've got so much support behind me. This is my chance.'"

We reached her office, a large room with a conference table, and sat to talk. "Why did you get into this work?" I asked.

"I'm from Brooklyn. I came to Chicago and fell in love—it's like a cleaner New York." She laughed. "But I was a teacher there, in schools near the Marcy Projects. I'd wanted to be a teacher since the second grade, when my teacher saw something in me and frequently asked me to help other kids in the class. I was like a little assistant and I was seven or eight years old. I was hooked. But mainly I got into it because I believe in supporting urban schools. Kids in typical inner-city schools don't have the same shot at getting the best teachers and principals. This is a rough area. I've interviewed people, and when they learn about the community they say, 'No. Not for me.' I get it. This year we've had two parents killed already. Just last week one of our pre-K babies"—"babies" was her preferred term for all of her students, no matter how old—"was shot while he was on the street with his whole family. He'll be all right, but this is a war zone. His brother and sisters come here too, and they're all traumatized.

"So I ask myself every day: Are we taking everything into account that these kids carry to school with them? That their parents carry around at home? I think AUSL does a good job of helping with those things. We have extra pieces throughout the building. We don't just drop a first-year teacher who's never taught black and brown kids into class and let her go. First, that teacher goes through a residency and then we provide support. Each and every day there are people giving you tips, coaching you, co-teaching.

We have two counselors in the building that AUSL provides. Other schools don't get that. It works."

We ended up speaking for at least an hour, and the more I listened to her, the more I thought about exactly how schools work. What are the things that I believe make schools work? What doesn't work? What can we identify and aspire to replicate? What are the lessons we can take away from the story of the Lewis School of Excellence, and many of the other stories found in this book?

The first lesson is that American families should have access to free, high-quality pre-K for every four-year-old. Every fall across the country we allow hundreds of thousands of five-year-old children to enter kindergarten who are one to two years behind. The brutal truth is that far too often these children *never* catch up. As a nation, we must get out of the catch-up game. We should provide every child with the opportunity to enter kindergarten possessing the academic, social, and emotional skills they need to be successful from day one. Everywhere I go, I say that the single best long-term investment for us to make would be in universal access to high-quality pre-K.

The second lesson, and one that the Lewis School provided gratis, is that after-school and enrichment programs should be provided to all students. This also speaks directly to my experience in Chicago, where we pioneered the After School Matters program with Maggie Daley. What I learned there is students want to stay in school to be with their friends, play games, learn new skills, and continue to grow in other ways outside the classroom but inside the school building. I also believe schools are vastly underutilized: they have auditoriums, gyms, libraries, cafeterias, industrial kitchens, ball fields, meeting rooms, swimming pools, projectors, musical instruments, and so many other physical assets that could be used twelve hours a day year-round to serve the community. I have no idea what the aggregate value of these are nationwide, but it must be in the trillions of dollars, and we should be proud of them. Schools also shouldn't offer enrichment just to students but to parents and the community at large. I would love to see a bigger push for community schools that open before classes begin and stay open long after they end, and that remain open all year. Parenting classes, GED and ESL courses, financial literacy programs, group therapy sessions, intramural sports, art classes, nutrition classes—all of these things and so many more can take place in our American schools. When schools become the heart of a community, and when parents and children learn together, great things happen.

The third lesson is that kids' social, emotional, and physical needs should be met by schools before their academic needs. That's the foundation. It's really hard to get a child who's hungry, afraid, sad, angry, or abused to learn if his more personal needs are not acknowledged and addressed. It goes right back to my mom's twenty-five pounds of apples and three pounds of cheese, and to her basic motto: "Any of us can learn. We just need consistent behavior and no violence. Care for the children. Care for the parents. Be honest. Be open. It works." Nowhere did she mention academics. Care was her number one priority.

The fourth lesson is that every school needs a great principal and every classroom a great teacher. When I served as secretary of education, I visited all different kinds of public schools: ones in inner-cities, in rural and remote areas, and on Native American reservations. Many of these schools were extraordinary. But I never once visited a great school that didn't also have a great principal. It isn't possible. Leadership matters, just like in any field. To get more great leaders in our schools, I believe we need to train, retain, and compensate our principals like the CEOs that they are. In turn, these great principals attract, nurture, and mentor great teachers, who are the ones doing the real, hard work every day.

The fifth lesson is that every high school student should graduate with some college credit, an industry certification, or both. Graduating from high school is an important accomplishment, but it's insufficient by itself; the goal is to prepare every student for success either in college or in the workplace.

The sixth lesson is that high schools need to do a better job of matching their graduates with colleges that are serious about graduating students just like them. Too many colleges are more interested in simply enrolling students than in seeing them walk across the stage after four, five, or even six or more years. The goal is never just to go to college and incur debt for no reason, it's to graduate.

The seventh lesson is that we must focus more on a PK–14 model as opposed to the current K–12 model. The demands of a twenty-first-century economy make this increasingly necessary.

Tennessee, under the leadership of Republican Governor Bill Haslam, recently made community college free for every Tennessean. Their goal is to get 55 percent of their citizens to have either a college degree or professional certificate by 2025, and they are moving in that direction. That's a model other states should replicate.

Lastly, I believe that every American citizen, even those who don't have children, should take the time to acknowledge that by every important metric our K–12 system ranks as average or below average compared to our industrialized peers. This is a true national crisis that for the most part goes unnoticed and unaddressed. One hundred years ago, America blazed a trail by mandating high school for every citizen. No other country had done this, and for decades afterward our educated workforce transformed what had been a middling economy into the largest and most vibrant one the world has ever seen. By some metrics, our economy has since been surpassed by China's, but for many ours remains the economic envy of the world. Other countries saw what we did and followed our lead, and now some have caught up. In terms of education, many have passed us. This should not be acceptable, yet we do accept it. When you consider that as recently as the 1980s we led the world in many educational metrics, it's even harder to accept. To take but one example, we were number one in college graduation rates roughly thirty years ago; now we're number sixteen. It's not so much that we've gotten worse, it's that we've flatlined and other countries are improving faster. They've done the necessary work to bring their teachers, schools, students, and educational systems into the twenty-first century. We've made strides in this direction—the movement the states undertook and the feds encouraged to raise standards has been an important step—but we have so much more to do. We cannot rest on our laurels and idly watch as other countries continue to eat our school lunch. Nothing short of our national security and economic future is at risk.

I mention national security for a reason. I often say that a strong military is our best defense, but that our educational system is our best offense. Our citizens and our leaders would never allow the United States not to have the world's best military, so why, then, do we allow ourselves to have a subpar educational system? Including higher education and across all levels of government, we spend a total of roughly $1 trillion a year on education, but this isn't enough. Our national security is measured not merely by tanks, aircraft carriers, and troops but also by our ability to generate and retain the world's most educated, most innovative, and most entrepreneurial citizenry. As impossible as it may sound, I'd like for us to spend twice as much on education—so long as we as educators are willing to hold ourselves accountable for better outcomes. I believe this investment would give untold returns, and that education is our best guarantor for American greatness over the long term. A smart and educated citizenry is the root strength of a democracy. It is also the source of all of our soft power, which has done as much or more to further the American ideal and creed than any of the wars we've waged. Furthermore, it's the source of our individual freedom. I mean that literally. Ask yourself who has more freedom, who has more options in his or her life: the person who dropped out of high school or the person who graduated from college? We debate endlessly the merits of spending a few thousand dollars to send one more child to pre-K, but think nothing of locking up one more adult at the cost of $75,000 per year. Why is that?

I believe that how schools do *not* work is the converse of the above: no support for pre-K or early education programs; no access to after-school programs or enrichment; a failure to meet the social and emotional needs of children; closing and locking a school's doors after the bell rings at three o'clock; pretending that teacher quality doesn't matter and that school leadership is unimportant; not giving high school students the ability to gain real skills *in* high school; and not bothering to place graduating high school seniors in postsecondary programs that meet their needs, abilities, and desires.

Ultimately, schools won't work if we refuse to believe in them or in their power to change lives. We *must* believe in free, high-quality public education. There is no substitute for it. And, while we have so much work to do to catch up with our international peers, we also have plenty of reasons to believe. Some would say otherwise, especially some in the current administration, but don't believe them. Education reform *is* working. There is never an end here; it's always a journey. There is always room for improvement, yet we have improved.

For example: since 1971, fourth-grade math and reading scores are up by 13 points and 25 points, respectively, and eighth-grade reading and math are up 8 points and 19 points, respectively. Every 10 points equals about a year's worth of learning, and a lot of the gains have been driven by black and brown students. The country is far more diverse and the public school student population is considerably poorer than in 1971, yet today's students are performing as much as two and a half grades *higher* than their peers from half a century ago.

More examples: the nation's high school graduation rate is at an all-time high of 84 percent. In 1980, only 23 percent of Americans aged twenty-five to twenty-nine had a four-year college degree; today 36 percent do, and over the same time period the percentage with a two-year degree has risen from 33 to 46 percent. African Americans and Latinos have increased their college-going numbers by an order of magnitude or more, and the total number of college students has risen from 8.6 million in 1993 to 12.5 million today.

None of this happened because we believed less in the power of education—it all happened because we believed in it *more*. If we want to further strengthen our schools and our educational system, then we have to keep believing, keep working, and keep holding ourselves, our students, our teachers, and our politicians to account. We cannot allow education to fall victim to the poison of our national divisions, and we have to support politicians willing to stand up to the status quo. During my career these have included people such as Mayor Daley, who embraced the idea that the educational buck stopped at his desk; they include President

Obama, who was willing to challenge his base even when he was politically vulnerable; they include Governor Kasich in Ohio, who continues to tout higher academic standards and has called the Republican outcry against the Common Core "hysteria . . . that is not well founded"; they include Governor Haslam in Tennessee, who has rejected his party's orthodoxy through his commitment to providing free community college to every Tennessean; and they include Governor Markell in Delaware, who during his time in office convened more than a dozen town halls to explain how they were not being honest with their students about what it meant to be college- and career-ready. Each of these were profiles in political courage, and whenever we, as voters, witness actions like these we should applaud and support them.

We also cannot allow those who call loudly for school choice—an idea I don't wholly discount, since I'm a firm believer in *good* and *accountable* public charter schools—to twist the debate into defunding public education, weakening unions, or allowing public dollars to fund private or faith-based schools. To continue to improve—and to get better at improving!—I firmly believe that we should set national goals. The federal government plays a limited role in national education policy, but this is where the Department of Education must take the lead. I watched my predecessors try to do just that, and I tried to do the same. It can and will happen again. This kind of leadership is also a component of how schools work.

Toward the end of my conversation with Mrs. Gonney-

Buckner at the Lewis School of Excellence, I asked her outright: "For you, how does school work?"

"You have to have people with the same vision," she said quickly, "the same level of buy-in. We all care here, for each other and for the kids. We don't always agree on specifics, but we share the same core values. We're all professionals—all of us, from myself to the teachers to the custodial staff to the security guards and the people in the cafeteria. We're all accountable. Also—" She cut herself off and took a few moments before continuing. "Arne," she said, "can I tell you a story about one of our students?"

"Absolutely."

"All right. His name is Gabriel. He's in the eighth grade. I mentioned the little pre-K baby who'd been shot?" I nodded. "That was his little brother. Gabriel was there when it happened. The shooter was retaliating for something their mother's boyfriend had done. All of them were together. Like I said, the little baby is going to be fine, and no one got killed, thank God.

"But Gabriel—he came to us in sixth grade. He's what's called a 'diverse learner': he was two or three years behind and had an IEP"—[an individualized education plan]—"A couple of months ago his grandma was here telling us about Gabriel. He'd been here two years already, but it was the first time we heard what she had to say. She told us that he and his siblings came to her because the police found them living at home alone when Gabriel was ten. He had three siblings, and he was taking care of all of them. Their mom would just disappear for days at a time and not leave any way to get in touch with her. There was no father in the house.

"That's when they came to live with Grandma, and that's when Gabriel and his siblings started coming here. They're still poor, but back then, when Gabriel was ten and needed money for food and diapers and things like that for his siblings, he would get up at four a.m. and go out and work. He just went out and asked convenience markets or guys doing paper routes if they needed help. Bagging groceries, odd jobs, that sort of thing. Whatever he could do, whatever he could make. Then, at eight thirty, he'd go off to school. Some days he didn't go to school at all. Who could blame him? He was doing whatever he had to do. He was *ten*.

"Now, Gabriel was a troublesome kid. When he got here he was getting into fights all the time, disrupting class, and making a scene in the hallway. But we stayed on him. We kept coming to him, talking to him. We consistently praised him when he did something right, and consistently took him aside when he didn't do something right. We'd ask him why he'd made the choice to act the way he had. It was constant and it came from all ends. Me, teachers, the janitors—anybody. Everyone knew about Gabriel. He was not unique in our school—we have an APB on all our babies at all times!—but he was still a special case. The main thing is that we paid attention to him. That goes a long way for a kid who's been neglected. 'How are you doing?' 'Are you okay?' These weren't things people asked him at home. He knew we cared, not only for him but for his friends and the other students too. He saw examples of good relationships all around him, and he started to think he wanted some of that too. 'Let me see what these people are all about,' he thought. You could see it. And he began to change.

"His baby brother, our pre-K baby, he was shot two days ago. And Gabriel hasn't been to school since. Again, how can I blame him? He's still in it. He's still living in this craziness. We want to give him the tools he needs to get out, to 'break the cycle of poverty'"—there was a large handwritten placard on the far side of the room that said exactly that as a daily reminder to Mrs. Gonney-Buckner and her team—"but he's not there yet.

"Now, when he *does* come back in here"—she slapped the table—"bam! We have a plan. As soon as Gabriel hits the ground, we'll have our counselor on deck. He'll do a peace circle right away with her." Earlier in our conversation she mentioned these as a kind of psychological debrief that students and sometimes parents got at the Lewis School. "The security guard will have him for the first two periods. I'll have him third and fourth. The lunch lady will sit with him in the cafeteria. And so on. He'll have someone with him at all times that day and for several days following. His classmates will know he needs support. This is what wraparound looks like! If you don't do these things, then you lose kids—end of story—and we can't afford to lose Gabriel. Think of what he'll be to the world—a boy who at ten got up at four to go to work in the dark of night so he could take care of his siblings! He had the courage to go out and ask strangers for a chance. He has CEO potential, and yet he's a below-grade-level black kid with special needs whom some other people would have just passed over without a second thought. Not us. Not here.

"How do schools work? By finding their Gabriels and running toward them. By being completely transparent and telling them constantly where they stand by using data, grades, and numbers. Gabriel and all of our kids know where they are at all times. We need to let them know both how far they have to go, and also how far they *can* go. School is concerned with a lot of numbers, but what we're really concerned with here are people. *That* is our business. And that is how *this* school works."

That says it all.

This is what it looks like when a school doesn't lie to its students. As Mrs. Gonney-Buckner spoke, I couldn't help but think of Calvin Williams, a victim of the system's lies whom I'd been unable to help enough all those years ago at the Sue Duncan Children's Center. Whatever would become of Gabriel, he was far less likely to suffer a similar fate. He would have Mrs. Gonney-Buckner, Ms. Malagic, and everyone at the Lewis School to thank for that.

We finished our conversation and I left the West Side, heading back to my office near the lake. I made sure to thank Mrs. Gonney-Buckner for everything she was doing. In my view, she, like all other great educators, is an American hero.

My closing plea is a simple one. It's that all of us care more about our American schools and the educational system that supports them. We need to stop lying to ourselves and be honest about what's at stake, and we need to face our challenges together.

With so much tearing us apart, I believe that the issue of education can bring us together in positive ways. That's a tired phrase overused by many politicians, but I'm not a politician and I mean it. I think that the best way we can be moved toward caring more is to be inspired. I hope that some of the things I've written about here have inspired you. But these stories are everywhere; they're in your hometown, your neighborhood, maybe even on your street. All you need to do is talk to people, ask questions, and listen.

I also believe we should talk to each other more so that we can set goals at all levels of government. Currently we don't have any. That's a failure of leadership. We can debate about what these goals should be, but for my part I'd set four objectives: As I've said, the first would be to provide access to high-quality public pre-K to all American children. The second would be to continue to make progress on high school graduation rates, hitting 90 percent nationwide in the next five years. The third would be to ensure that 100 percent of our high school graduates are college- and career-ready—we need to stop lying about what this means and stop handing out meaningless diplomas. And the fourth would be that we commit once again to leading the world in college graduation rates. If we could come together to meet these goals, this could also be a source of inspiration, regardless of which party you support.

Individually, my fervent hope is that the next time each of us steps into the voting booth, we think of education. Politicians at all levels—from local school boards to mayors to governors to members of Congress and all the way to the occupant of the Oval

Office—must be held accountable for improving educational outcomes. When presidential candidates debate, they're hardly ever asked about education, even though it's a critical component of our national and economic security. That is wrong. Ensuring that we have a strong education system is the only way to build a strong and vibrant middle class, and it is vital to a healthy and functioning democracy. Our public schools should not be so easy to forget and not care about. If we continue to not care, or to allow our leaders to lure us into political fights that lead nowhere, then our schools will continue to suffer. They will not improve, they will not work, and the lies will continue to flourish. We *must* care. It isn't only the future of our children that's at stake. It is the future of our country.

APPENDIX

WHAT CAN YOU DO?

I'd like to close by urging all voters—parents and non-parents alike—to think about the following questions when they think about schools, teachers, and education, and whenever they interact with politicians and our leaders in media and government:

I. **Why don't all kids have access to early learning?** This is the most basic and fundamental measure of our commitment to students. If we're not getting kids into preschool, then we're simply not serious about closing achievement gaps. While we've made some gains at the local level, we're not remotely close to getting the job done. Other countries do so much more to prepare their young children for a life of learning.

II. **What are we doing to get the best teachers and principals in front of the neediest students?** As I've written in these pages, the most important in-school factor in a child's life is the quality of their teacher. Currently, there isn't a single US school district that systematically identifies their most successful teachers and principals, nor are there any that encourage these experts to work with their neediest children. If we did nothing but address this failure, we could transform public education in America.

III. **Why can't schools offer more time and services to our children and their communities?** Almost without exception, all of our high-performing public schools serving at-risk kids find ways to provide more time in school. Many districts don't do this and the result is that our kids suffer. There should be no one-size-fits-all amount of time spent at school. Some kids need six hours. Some need eight, and some need twelve or more as well as three meals a day. Some need school year-round, some don't. That there's no flexibility here, and that time spent in school is for the most part a constant as opposed to a variable, is wrong. The truth is that many kids, especially poorer ones regardless of race, don't just need more school, they also *want* it. We should be doing everything possible to give it to them.

IV. **How many of our young adults finish college, and what's our national goal?** In the United States, about 70 percent of wealthier students complete college, when only about 9 percent of poorer students do. This is a staggering difference that perpetuates our national crises of wealth disparity and the lack of economic mobility. Today in America, talent is more evenly distributed than opportunity; for a country that's supposed to be the world's leading democracy, that's not just wrong, it's immoral. Other countries are doing so much more to increase college graduation rates across all levels of society. We must set similar, more ambitious goals. Our economy and our society cannot remain competitive with so much squandered talent and so many undereducated Americans.

V. **How can I change the way I think about education?** Think of your local public schools, including your state's public community colleges and research universities, as your personal property—because they are. Their quality affects you, your children, your home's value, your community, your state, and your country. No other public investment is more closely tied to the American Dream than the quality of education in *your* community. Act like it. Support public school teachers. Support community colleges. Support public universities. Demand more resources and more accountability from everyone. Demand better access to higher education. Above all, keep fighting for education, and never stop.

INDEX

ABOUT THE AUTHOR

ARNE DUNCAN was born and raised in Chicago, Illinois. He was CEO of the Chicago Public Schools from 2001 to 2008, and served in President Barack Obama's cabinet as secretary of education from 2009 to 2015. He and his family returned to Chicago in 2016. He is now a managing partner at the nonprofit Emerson Collective, where he works on projects throughout the city to reduce gun violence. This is his first book.